STUDIES
IN
JEWISH DREAM
INTERPRETATION

STUDIES
IN
JEWISH DREAM
INTERPRETATION

MONFORD HARRIS

JASON ARONSON INC.
Northvale, New Jersey
London

The author gratefully acknowledges permission to reprint from the following sources:

From MINHAT YEHUDAH by Judah Ftayya, copyright © 1955–1956 by Shaul Ftayya. Used by permission.

From EXODUS AND EXILE by Monford Harris, pp. 79–84. Copyright © 1992 by Augsburg Fortress. Used by permission.

From THE INTERPRETATION OF DREAMS IN THE ANCIENT NEAR EAST by A. Leo Oppenheim, copyright © 1956 by the American Philosophical Society. Used by permission.

Adaptation of "Dreams in Sefer Hasidim" by Monford Harris, published in *Proceedings of the American Academy of Jewish Research* 31(1963): 51–80. Copyright © 1963 by the American Academy of Jewish Research. Used by permission.

Adaptation from PERSPECTIVES IN JEWISH LEARNING, vol. 1, edited by Monford Harris, pp. 23–43. Copyright © 1965 by the College of Jewish Studies. Used by permission of Spertus Institute of Jewish Studies.

All translations of talmudic passages are from the Soncino translation, unless otherwise noted.

This book was set in 11 pt. Schneidler by Lind Graphics of Upper Saddle River, New Jersey, and printed and bound by Haddon Craftsmen of Scranton, Pennsylvania.

Library of Congress Cataloging-in-Publication Data

Harris, Monford, 1920–
    Studies in Jewish dream interpretation / by Monford Harris.
        p. cm.
    Includes bibliographical references and index.
    ISBN 1-56821-126-0
    1. Dreams — Religious aspects — Judaism.   2. Dream interpretation in rabbinical literature.   3. Rabbinical literature — History and criticism.   I. Title.
    BF1078.H295   1994
    154.6′3′089924 — dc20   93-38060

Manufactured in the United States of America. Jason Aronson Inc. offers books and cassettes. For information and catalog write to Jason Aronson Inc., 230 Livingston Street, Northvale, New Jersey 07647.

To
Rivkah

Loving Learned Wise

CONTENTS

ACKNOWLEDGMENTS

I am gratefully indebted to many generous people:

To the staff of the Helen Asher–Norman Asher Library of Spertus College of Judaica: Michael Terry, director, for his courtesies; Chava Feferman for her graciously given technical help and knowledge of many things; Robbin Katzin for locating volumes; Kathy Ladien for technical assistance; Ahuvah Rosenberg for Hebrew typing; Dan Sharon for so generously sharing with me his bibliographical knowledge; and to the part-time members of the library staff.

To Mrs. Rosaline Cohn for the grant from the Cohn Scholars Fund of Spertus College, which was helpful in the process of publication;

To Dr. Byron L. Sherwin, vice-president for academic affairs, for his courtesies;

To Reva Slaw, college bursar, for her helpfulness;

To Marshall Wolke for his suggested translations from Yiddish;

To Pamela Spitzner, secretary to the vice-president for academic affairs and to the faculty, for her superb secretarial skills, for her patience with me, for reading my hieroglyphic manuscript, and for her promptness in processing it;

To Rivkah for her help and encouragement.

INTRODUCTION

The Jewish dream interpretations in this book, coming from different times and places, and different as each is from the other, nevertheless share certain basic assumptions.

Important for Jewish oneirocritics is the idea that "all dreams follow the mouth" of the interpreter, first formulated in tractate *Berakhot* of the Talmud, but, as suggested there, already implicit in the biblical account of Joseph's interpreting the dreams of Pharaoh and the two servants. This idea is sometimes only implicit as, for instance, in the nineteenth- and twentieth-century work of the traditional Iraqi Judah Ftayya and explicit in the early twentieth-century Yiddish *Interpretation of Dreams* by a secular oneirocritic in New York.

Of importance for the dream interpreters, except for the secularist, was the hermeneutics of the Word. Despite the fact that dreams are visual phenomena, Jewish dream interpretation interprets things seen in dreams as thing = word seen in the dream. Jewish dream interpretation, therefore, is, for the most part, a kind of text analysis. It was not adventitious that Judah Ftayya included his oneirocriticism in the book devoted to biblical interpretation.

Joseph, the first "Jewish" oneirocritic, is mentioned only in passing in the works studied, possibly for a number of reasons. Joseph interpreted only four dreams: the dream of the butler, the dream of the baker, and the two dreams of Pharaoh. And these dreamers were Gentiles. Jewish oneirocritics interpret dreams of Jews, although in the Talmud, in the Midrash, and in *Sefer Hasidim* sages do, on occasion, interpret dreams of Gentiles. Joseph indicated that he was not an oneirocritic when he proclaimed that interpretations come from God (Genesis 40:8; 41:16, 25). Joseph was only an emissary. And, at that, only in two instances: once in a prison and once in a palace.

Joseph was, however, of some consequence to the outstanding oneirocritic of the twentieth century. Ken Frieden's learned and stimulating *Freud's Dream of Interpretation* discusses Joseph's import for Freud:

> Freud admits to identifying with the biblical Joseph. Yet as a modern interpreter he rejects what he takes to be Joseph's archaic methods . . . Although Freud renounces the earlier methods, then in some respects he does identify with his ancient precursors Joseph and Artemidoros. Apart from their common interpretive activity, Freud may also have identified with Joseph as a result of their similar position in the family romance. As favored first sons of Jacob's second wife, they received special privileges . . . Joseph's approach to dream interpretation becomes clearer in relation to that of Sigmund Freud, whose *Interpretation of Dreams* refers to Joseph several times. Freud observes that in his own dreams, because of the biblical prototype, characters named Joseph often stand for Freud himself.[1]

In the works studied here – the Talmud, *Sefer Hasidim*, Rabbi Solomon Almoli's sixteenth-century *Interpretation of Dreams*, Rabbi Judah Ftayya's dream interpretations, secular A. B.'s *Interpretation of Dreams*, *Encyclopedia Talmudit*'s articles on dreams, Rabbi Halevi's study of the Priestly Blessing, the traditional dream therapy prayers–Joseph as oneirocritic is of marginal interest or is totally ignored. For Freud, however, Joseph was of personal significance and of some academic interest. This is a paradox worth pondering.

The prayer concerning dreams recited during the Priestly Blessing refers to *healing* twice, citing three biblical persons cured from their illnesses: Miriam, King Hezekiah, and Naaman. Solomon Almoli, the most important traditional oneirocritic by virtue of his book's comprehensiveness and its popularity, was not only a rabbinical jurist but also a doctor of medicine. And Ftayya, while not a physician, was a therapist, curing people possessed by evil spirits.

Isaac ben Judah Abrabanel (1437–1508), statesman, philosopher, and biblical exegete, devoted a number of pages in his commentary to the Pentateuch to Joseph's dream interpretations. Reflecting on the oneirocritic he wrote:

> I think that the [dream] interpreter is in general like the doctor who heals diseases. For just as the doctor heals them [the diseases] when they are hidden from him in the body of the person by means of the signs of the pulse, the urine and other things, so [too] the interpreter interprets and tells what the soul of the dreamer saw by the emanation that emanated upon it, a matter hidden from him [the interpreter] by means of the signs he sees and [of what] he hears from the recounting of his [the dreamer's] dream.[2]

Abrabanel's proposal is interesting not only by virtue of the coincidence in the person of Freud. It is suggestive of the Jewish tradition in which dream interpretation has always been involved with healing, of ridding the dreamer of his/her anxieties.

These studies, although for the most part chronologically arranged, do not imply a Comtian progression from a mythical stage, to a metaphysical stage, to a positivist stage of postclassical halakhists or a secular Jewish oneirocriticism. No cumulative knowledge is implied by the arrangement of these studies. They are discrete studies of Jewish traditions of dream interpretation.

1

THE PRIMARY SOURCES

Hebrew Scripture and Talmud, the two primary works of classical, that is, traditional, Judaism, are bonded together. Scripture was canonized, organized, and vocalized by the sages so as to be acquired by the community. And the Talmud emerged from the matrix of Scripture. Both have references to dreams.

In the this-worldly piety of biblical-rabbinic Judaism, the oneiric realm is only of relative importance. Dreams occur only during sleep, and sleep in Jewish tradition, as in other traditions, is considered "one sixtieth part of death."[1] This association of sleep with death is noteworthy because "the social nothingness of sleep implied by the comparison with death . . . points to absence of interaction and social isolation."[2] Furthermore, during sleep there is "the suspension of historical continuity, the disintegration of spatial and temporal ordering, the vagueness of identity."[3] For Jewish tradition in which social interaction, historical continuity, distinct identity, and spacial and temporal ordering are crucial, dreams occurring during sleep would not be of central importance.

Nevertheless, human beings do dream. And as Scripture deals

with the dreams of kings and others so, too, the Talmud has references to dreams.[4]

Scripture's most important dreamer was Joseph, whose two dreams served a twofold purpose: to indicate his destiny and to stimulate his brothers' hostility. Neither he nor his brothers were in need of interpretation. Joseph may not have been fully aware of the dream's meaning. Perhaps here, as in many a narrative, Scripture is intentionally elusive. But his brothers understood the implications of the dreams. Years later Joseph's encounter with Pharaoh's cupbearer and baker, whose respective dreams he interpreted, leads to his being summoned to interpret Pharaoh's dreams. Scripture implies that in the process of his interpretation of those two dreams, Joseph began to understand the meaning of his own dreams. His unsolicited astute counsel to Pharaoh (Genesis 41:33–36) was also his interpretation of his own two dreams.

The magnificent Joseph narrative, only one strand of which refers to Joseph's oneirocritical skills, serves primarily to bring the Israelites into Egypt. Joseph as oneirocritic is never referred to again.

The other important dream interpreter in Scripture is Daniel, who interpreted Nebuchadnezzar's dreams and his own dreams.[5]

Neither Joseph nor Daniel joins those who regularly serve to interpret their respective king's dreams. Neither is a career oneirocritic.

There are, of course, other dreamers in Hebrew Scripture. Jacob, Joseph's father, had a dream on the way to Haran of a ladder from earth to the heavens with ascending and descending angels and God standing beside Jacob, assuring him that his descendants would inherit the land (Genesis 28:12–15). Another dreamer is that Midianite soldier telling his comrade of his dream of a barley cake knocking over a Midianite tent, which cues in Gideon to the Israelites' coming victory (Judges 7). And there is Solomon's dream in which he is promised wisdom (1 Kings 3:5–15).[6]

In the Pentateuch, a work containing many regulations about many things, there are no rules, regulations, or laws about dreams. In all of Hebrew Scripture there are only narratives about dreams of some individuals because of their importance in the context of historical events. Indeed, in Hebrew Scripture there is no reference to an office of Israelite oneirocritic.

The Talmud focuses on dreams primarily in tractate *Berakhot*. In chapter 9, known as *Ha-Ro'eh*, "One Who Sees," there are presented blessings to be recited on seeing certain phenomena both natural, such as mountains, deserts, and rainbows, and historical, such as the collapsed walls of Jericho and the salt pillar that was Lot's wife. But this chapter, the locus classicus of talmudic dream material, has no blessing to be recited on having seen a dream.

One might assume that the Talmud so inextricably bonded to Scripture would, in tractate *Berakhot*, discuss Joseph *the* biblical dream interpreter. Joseph is referred to as one over whom the evil eye had no power; as assuming airs of authority; from whose experiences (Genesis 37:9) one learns that only part of a dream might be fulfilled, never the whole dream; that it may take as long as twenty-two years for a dream to be fulfilled (Genesis 41:46); that had Potiphar not appointed Joseph as majordomo he would not have had trouble; and the "dream of Joseph" is mentioned in the Priestly Blessing service.[7] But Joseph is never referred to as dream interpreter. He is not the Talmud's paradigmatic oneirocritic. Indeed, in the Talmud there is no paradigmatic oneirocritic. There are, however, sages who, among their other activities, did interpret dreams as shall be noted.

There is no systematic *analysis* of dreams, nor are any rules formulated for dream interpretation. In this and other chapters of *Berakhot* and other tractates of the Talmud, there are many different reports and observations about dreams. Most aphorisms and adages are stated without further ado. Rabbi Zera's dictum, "Whoever goes seven days without a dream is called evil,"[8] is not explored. But such observations must have been the products of much thinking about the subject of dreams.

Rabbi Hisda no doubt reflected on the nature of dreams, for a number of observations are attributed to him. He opined that "neither a good dream nor a bad dream is ever wholly fulfilled," but "a bad dream is better than a good dream," presumably because it encourages one to repent. He was so concerned with one's response to dreams that he concluded that "the sadness caused by a bad dream is sufficient for it and the joy which a good dream gives is sufficient for it." But Hisda also appreciated the dreamer's fright: "A bad dream is worse than scourging." His most important dictum because of the metaphor that he uses and because it implies the role of interpretation is his apothegm, "A dream which is not interpreted is like a letter which is not read."[9]

Other maxims by various *amoraim* (postmishnaic sages) are presented in a kind of tessellation of dream interpretations. A fragment is contributed by R. Johanan in the name of R. Simon b. Yohai: "Just as wheat cannot be without straw so there cannot be a dream without some nonsense." And "A man should await the fulfillment of a dream for as much as twenty-two years."[10]

Rabbi Huna's observation adds to the mosaic of dream material and is reassuring, at least for some dreamers: "A good person [the Hebrew *adam*, which can be a bisexual term since Hebrew has no neuter nouns–cf. Genesis 5:2] is not shown a good dream and a bad person is not shown a bad dream,"[11] meaning that the good person is being encouraged to repent for his misdeeds, the bad person rewarded for having done some good. This insight is buttressed by biblical verses.

As part of the configuration of dream material, R. Huna bar Ammi referred to a teaching he received from R. Pedath, who in turn had received it from R. Johanan: the Amelioration of Dreams service. That the sages had received the tradition from another sage who in turn had received it from another indicates that this teaching had an authoritative character, which, of course, accounts for its subsequent incorporation into the traditional prayer book.[12]

These teachings in the Talmud do not have the authority of the *halakhah*, but they are not idle musings. They constitute traditional wisdom despite the *apparent* informality of the situation in which they were stated. This is particularly true in the following account: Three sages, "Amemar, Mar Zutra, and R. Ashi were once sitting together. They said, 'Let each of us say something which his colleague has not heard.' " Who said what is not recorded. One tells what a person who fears an Evil Eye should do on entering a city. Another explains what one who becomes ill should *not* do in order to avoid the Evil Eye. And the third sage tells the other two the prayer concerning dreams to be recited during the Priestly Blessing in the synagogue.[13]

As if the redactors of the Talmud intended a dialectical treatment of dream importance, they inserted the following immediately after the three sages' discussion: "When Samuel had a bad dream he used to say, 'The dream speaks falsely' [quoting Zechariah 10:2]; when he had a good dream, he used to say, 'Do the dreams speak falsely seeing that it is written, "I [God] do speak with him in a dream" ' " (Numbers 12:6). To this is added Rava's observation that these verses contradict each other and his resolution of the contradiction, that the first verse refers to dreams via a demon and the second to dreams via an angel. Rava leaves it at that without giving criteria for distinguishing between the two kinds of dreams.[14]

The Talmud complicates the subject of dreams and develops a problematic of dream interpretaton. For there follows what is perhaps the most intriguing statement about the subject of dreams in the entire rabbinic tradition:

> R. Bizna b. Zabda said in the name of R. Akiba who had it from R. Panda who had it from R. Nahum, who had it from R. Biryam reporting a certain elder – and who was this? R. Bana'ah: There were twenty-four interpreters of dreams in Jerusalem. "Once I dreamt a dream and I went round to all of them and they all gave different interpretations, and all were fulfilled, thus confirming that which is said: All dreams follow the mouth." Is the statement that all dreams follow the mouth Scriptural? Yes, as stated by R. Eleazar. For R. Eleazar said: "Whence do we know that all dreams follow the mouth? Because it says, *and it came to pass, as he interpreted to us, so it was.*" Raba said: "This is only if the interpretation corresponds to the content of the dream: for it says, *to each man according to his dream he did interpret. When the chief baker saw that the interpretation was good.*" How did he know this? R. Eleazar says: "This tells us that each of them was shown his own dream and the interpretation of the other one's dream."[15]

Aside from the critical issue in this passage, to be discussed subsequently, there are other interesting aspects. There was, it is indicated, an enduring tradition about an experience that a late *tanna* – early *amora*, Rabbi Bana'ah, the head of the Academy at Tiberias, had. It was important enough to have been transmitted through five sages, each of whom memorized it or perhaps recorded it in his "notebook," a not infrequent practice then. Also interesting is the fact that R. Bana'ah's experience is transmitted in the first person; *he* tells of his experience.

The critical issue is the reference to the twenty-four dream interpreters giving twenty-four different interpretations of the same dream. Could there have been twenty-four oneirocritics in Jerusalem at the close of the third century c.e.? This number, however, should be taken *cum grano salis*. It occurs with some frequency in the rabbinic tradition. In reference to Jerusalem it may suggest plenitude. According to Rabbi Samuel, "There were twenty-four thoroughfares in Jerusalem. Each thoroughfare had twenty-four side turnings; each side turning had twenty-four streets; each street had twenty-four houses." And in the Jerusalem temple, "a bull was offered by twenty-four priests."[16]

Rabbi Bana'ah made the rounds of the Jerusalem oneirocritics for their interpretations. Was it that he wanted "another expert's opinion" each time, or did he hope for a better interpretation each time? Whatever the nature of his dream, he must have achieved much if all "twenty-four" interpretations were fulfilled.

R. Bana'ah's statement that "all were fulfilled, thus confirming that which is said 'All dreams follow the mouth'" *implies* that the conception, though not the quotation, is scriptural. The Talmud makes this implication explicit. It raises the question, "Is the statement that all dreams follow the mouth, scriptural?" And it answers it in the affirmative: "Yes, as stated by R. Eleazar. For R. Eleazar said: Whence do we know that all dreams follow the mouth? Because it says, 'And it came to pass as he [Joseph] interpreted it to us so it was'" (Genesis 41:13).

The "twenty-four" Jerusalem oneirocritics were obviously not Freudian, Jungian, Adlerian, or Binswangerian in their dream interpretation. What were they? R. Bana'ah did not say, nor did he record their interpretations. There can be no doubt, however, that they belonged to the same "school" of interpretation: biblical hermeneutics. We shall return to this issue.

The chapter entitled "One Who Sees" continues with a melange of dream interpretations by some forty or so rabbinic sages, and, in a way, this constitutes a kind of dream manual that the learned down the generations may have consulted once the Talmud was canonized. The sages whose interpretations of dreams are recorded in this chapter of tractate *Berakhot* are not given in any particular sequence of chronology or importance.[17]

Rabbi Ishmael (ben Ishmael) interpreted his nephew ben Dama's dream of jaws falling out as signifying an unsuccessful plot by two Roman counselors, foiled by their demise. This is followed by the report of Bar Kappara telling Rabbi [Judah ha-Nasi, the redactor of the Mishnah] of his four dreams: his nose falling off, his hands cut off, his legs cut off, and he would die in the month of *Adar*. R. Judah interpreted them favorably.[18]

More interpretations by R. Ishmael follow. A sectarian's[19] fourteen dreams were interpreted by him. Two were interpreted as referring to the man's crimes done to Jews, one as referring to his dismissal of two wives without divorcing them, and one as the man's having stripped a corpse. Nine other dreams were interpreted as the man's having been involved with sexual transgressions. The sectarian admits the validity of the interpretations except the one of stripping the corpse. That interpretation, however, is verified by a woman who intruded on the two men. And one dream was about people telling the sectarian that his deceased father had left him money in Cappadocia. After questioning the man and learning that the man did not have money there, nor had his deceased father even been in Cappadocia, Ishmael told the man to examine the tenth beam in order to find money. The interpretation turned out to be right.[20] Noteworthy is Ishmael's questioning his client; interpretation presupposes some discussion with the client. This may have occurred more frequently than the texts indicate.

There follows in this chapter of *Berakhot* various statements about dream interpretation by sundry rabbis. A water well seen in a dream is interpreted in three different ways. Rabbi Hanina says it signifies *place* on the basis of Genesis 26:19 with its reference to finding a well of "living waters." According to R. Nathan it means *Torah* on the basis of Proverbs 8:35, "Whoso findeth me findeth life" and Torah is a well of living water. For Rava, *well* means "life, literally."[21]

R. Hanan was of the opinion that three things seen in a dream—a river, a bird, and a pot—mean place, on the basis of Isaiah 31:5, where birds and God's protection are both mentioned, and Isaiah 26:12, with its reference to *establishing*, which can also mean "placing a pot on a fire," and to *peace*.[22]

R. Joshua ben Levi, more concerned about immediate therapy

than interpretation, advised early rising after a dream and reciting certain positive biblical verses rather than others that might occur to the person on arising.[23]

This is followed by what "Our Rabbis Taught," interpreting the meanings of different things, for example, reeds, a pumpkin, wax, ox, and so forth, and sundry observations about other objects seen in dreams. An ass means salvation on the basis of Zechariah 9:9; a cat means a beautiful song in a locale where cat is called *shunara*, but where it is called *shinra* it indicates change for the worse, interpretations that are paronomastic. Different-colored grapes have different meanings, as do various animals, biblical personalities, personal names.

Some erotic dreams are interpreted. Intercourse with one's mother means that one will acquire understanding, an interpretation based on Proverbs 2:3, "Yea, if those call for understanding," which is vocalized to read "Yea, you will call understanding mother," by changing a vowel point of the Hebrew *if* (*im*) so that it is read *mother* (*aim*). A dream of intercourse with a maiden betrothed to another means that one will acquire knowledge of Torah on the basis of Deuteronomy 33:4, "Torah [an *inheritance, morashah*] is vocalized to read *me'orasah*, betrothed." Intercourse with one's sister means that one will obtain wisdom on the basis of Proverbs 7:4, "Say unto wisdom, 'Thou art my sister.' " One who dreams of intercourse with a married woman can be certain that he will be a denizen of the world-to-come.[24] Evidently, sharing another's wife indicates that in paradise he will enjoy his and the other's portion. This is Rashi's explanation, which implies, at least, that the enjoyment of a forbidden sexual pleasure points to the pleasure of paradise. That is the meaning of this dream of adultery, only on the condition, however, that the dreamer did not know the woman or had not thought of the woman that evening.

The interpretations of these erotic dreams, two violating incest laws, one a kind of adultery, and one a clear case of adultery, are somewhat surprising considering the Talmud's value system. Curiously, while intercourse with a *married* woman was interpreted, dreaming of intercourse with a woman is not mentioned.

This last chapter of *Berakhot* continues with various sages interpreting things seen in dreams. Rabbi Hiyya ben Abba interpreted wheat as indicating peace on the basis of Psalm 147:14, in which peace and wheat occur; barley in a dream means one's sins will depart on the basis of Isaiah 6:7, "thine iniquity is taken away [*sar avon* is vocalized as *se'orim*, that is, barley]. Two different vines seen in a dream, a fig tree, pomegranates in various conditions, different olives, and palm trees are all interpreted favorably using biblical verses.[25]

Rabbi Joseph interpreted a goat or several goats as blessings on the basis of Proverbs 27:27, and a myrtle as success in property holdings because myrtle has many lives.[26]

Other interpretations, using biblical verses or wordplay, are given. A goose signifies wisdom because of Proverbs 1:20, "Wisdom crieth aloud in the streets." Rav Ashi gives personal testimony to the validity of this interpretation. Also interpreted are a cock, several cocks, a hen, eggs, different animals, colors, utensils, and other objects used in an agrarian economy; most of them are interpreted favorably. There are also dreams interpreted as indicating professional advancement for sages.[27] Many symbols are interpreted not on the basis of biblical verses but by association of ideas.

Dreams about biblical personalities – David, Solomon, Ahab – are interpreted, as are dreams of biblical books – Book of Kings, Ezekiel, Jeremiah, Isaiah, Psalms, Proverbs, Job, Song of Songs, Lamentations, Scroll of Esther. But dreams about the pentateuchal books or pentateuchal personalities ar not interpreted, which is rather surprising.[28]

Dreams of an erotic nature are rarely recorded. Aside from the four erotic dreams that we noted, there is, in this chapter, a dream that we would consider erotic but the sages did not: "He who stands naked in a dream, [if] in Babylon he stands [naked] he is sinless; [if] in the Land of Israel, [he is] bereft of the pieties."[29] The interpretation of naked-in-Babylon presupposes a rabbinic dictum that living outside of the Land of Israel is as if one worshiped idols,[30] hence being naked in Babylon means not being "clothed" in sins; being naked in the Land of Israel, where one does not worship idols, means that one is stripped of the pieties. Nakedness, depending on the locale, signifies pious/impious.

This last chapter of *Berakhot* also contains the account of Bar Hedya, *the* oneirocritic, eventually put to death by torsion, and of his two clients, the sages Rava and Abaye, which we shall discuss in the chapter "Ambivalence."

Some forty sages are referred to as dreamers and/or as interpreters

of dreams. Practically all of the interpretations of the things seen in
dreams are favorable for the dreamer, because ridding the dreamer of
his anxiety was interpretation's function. There is no theoretical analysis of the nature of dreams. No sage raises any questions about the
"twenty-four" Jerusalem oneirocritics and their different interpretations. The sages did not raise questions about them because for the
sages Torah, which includes the Pentateuch and the other Hebrew
scriptural books and the oral teachings, in its plenitude has many
meanings. And the sages, and no doubt the twenty-four dream interpreters among whom there may have been sages such as Bar Hedya,
turned to Scripture for the interpretation of dreams. Saul Lieberman, in
his classic study *Hellenism in Jewish Palestine*, says, "The entire rabbinic
literature bears testimony to the fact that the Rabbis knew the Bible by
heart, Jerome testifies that the Palestinian Jews of the fourth century
were able to recite the Pentateuch and the Prophets by heart."[31] This
served them in interpreting dreams, even at times when it was necessary to change a jot or a tittle of the biblical verse. Torah, the ultimate
source of traditional knowledge, was also therefore the source for
dream interpretation.

An anonymous midrash makes this point in a curiously reversed
way:

> "Behold," it says, "A dream carries much implication." [Ecclesiastes 5:2]
> Now by using the method of kal vahomer (a minori ad maius) we
> reason: If the contents of dreams which have no effect may yield a
> multitude of interpretations, how much more then should the impor-
> tant contents of the Torah imply many interpretations in every verse.[32]

This midrash likens dream interpretations to Torah interpretations,
which implies that just as Torah is text and has many interpretations,
so dreams are texts the interpreter reads, and their "words" (*divrey*;
Lieberman translated as "contents") may yield a multitude of interpretations.

This accounts for the "twenty-four" different interpretations by
those Jerusalem oneirocritics. These different interpretations were all
implicit in Torah texts, which one may assume they used, although
this was not recorded, for their respective interpretations. One may

assume this because early on in the development of the rabbinic tradition it was said, "Turn it and turn it again for everything is in it."[33]

The study of Scripture, a major activity of the rabbis, made them most sensitive to words. And their dream interpretation was a *reading of the words* for the objects seen in the dream, even of words never found in Scripture. The word *cat* does not occur in all of Hebrew Scripture, but Scripture so influenced these sages that a cat in a dream leads them to interpreting the *word* cat: in one region the *word*, not the animal, is interpreted as "beautiful song," in another as "evil change."

That the *word* for the object serves as the basis for interpretation is a biblical point of view is obvious early on in the book of the first of the literary prophets, Amos. In his vision of a basket of summer fruit, Amos responds to God's query that he sees a basket of summer fruit. These two (Hebrew) words that he utters are then interpreted paronomastically by God as meaning "the end" (a wordplay on summer fruit).[34] The object, summer fruit, is not the message. The Hebrew *word* for summer fruit is the message.

The distinction that we make between object and word is, however, not biblical but rather a distinction made by moderns, heirs of the medieval debate between the nominalists and the realists. The biblical view is different. Since for the rabbinic sages the Bible was central, Johannes Pedersen's study of the biblical outlook is instructive. In reflecting on the *words* of the blessing he wrote:

> Thus no distinction is made between the word and the matter described, and consequently, the Hebrew denominations of a word may just as well apply to the matter . . . For the Israelite there is upon the whole no difference whatsoever between the idea, the name, and the matter itself.[35]

Interpreting the object is, therefore, interpreting the word. Dream interpretation is an interpretation of the object-which-is-word that is seen.

In his *Interpretation of Dreams in the Ancient Near East*, A. Leo Oppenheim found it

> tempting to speculate whether the Talmudic concept of a supernatural dispenser of dreams, the ba'al halom, reflects in any way the Mesopota-

mian tradition of a Dream-god. The very fact that the Palestinian version of the Talmud does not mention this angelic figure lends some weight to this theory.[36]

Oppenheim wisely left it at that, for this "talmudic concept" of a supernatural dispenser of dreams is of such minor importance in the Talmud that it can hardly be considered a rabbinic concept. Neither is the *ba'al halom* of any significance in posttalmudic literature.

The first occurrence of *ba'al halom* is in the Book of Genesis. Joseph sent by his father to inquire of his brothers' welfare is espied by them as he approaches: "And they saw him afar off and before he came near unto them they conspired against him to slay him. And they said to one another: 'Behold this *ba'al ha-halomot* cometh.' "[37] Here, of course, this term (*halomot* is the plural of *halom*) refers to Joseph the dreamer and it is used derisively.

In the Talmud there are only two references[38] to the supernatural *ba'al halom*:

> If one felt distressed over some money which his father had left him [since it may have been tithe money] and the ba'al halom appeared to him and named the sum, indicated the place and specified its purpose, saying that it was [for the redemption] of the second tithe—such an incident once occurred, and they [the rabbis on that occasion] said, "Dreams are of no account."[39]

The other reference to *ba'al halom* in the Talmud is the following: "Rabbi Hanan said, 'Even if the ba'al ha'-halomot says to a person [*adam* in Hebrew] that on the morrow he will die, he should not desist from prayer; for so it says 'For in the multitude of dreams are vanities and also many words; but fear thou God' " (Ecclesiastes 5:6).[40]

There are also a few references to the *ba'al halom* in other early rabbinic texts. In the *Tosefta* an *ish halom*, a (supernatural) dream dispenser came

> to one who was concerned about his deceased father's apportioned second tithe and told him where it was to be found. Although it was found as the Ish Halom said it would be, the sages declared that it was not tithed grain because "Dreams are of no account."[41]

In *Avot d'Rabbi Nathan* the *ba'al halom* warns a "Greek" to free a Jewish maiden reared by him. He finally frees her.[42]

The same story, with minor variations, is recorded in *Midrash Tannaim.*[43]

In *Midrash Shir Ha-Shirim* there is an account of the *ba'al halom* appearing in a dream to a man troubled by his wife whose very name was Grace and whose demeanor was graceful but whose face was ugly. On being told by the dreamer that the ugliness troubled him, the *ba'al halom* asked whether he wanted his wife to be attractive. He affirmed that he did. The next morning, having become attractive, the woman was haughty toward her husband. That night the *ba'al halom* appeared. The husband requested that his wife return to her former ugliness and her gracious behavior. This was granted.[44] The same story is reported in *Midrash Ha-Gadol.*[45]

In *Sefer Hasidim*, the medieval work produced by the devout of Germany, the *ba'al halom* is referred to twice. The first is incidental, "like a *ba'al halom* coming to one in a dream." The other reference is noteworthy. It warns that if the *ba'al ha-halomot* will tell a dreamer to violate the *mitzvot* (the divinely instituted pieties), the dreamer should not hearken to him.[46]

That the *ba'al halom* might appear to a dreamer tempting him to impious acts is not only criticism but a rejection of the *ba'al halom*, who, at least in this account, is an antinomian figure.

Solomon Almoli, in his sixteenth-century *Interpretation of Dreams*, states:

> The interpreter of dreams should know that a dream that one has because one thought about such a matter during the day or was involved with such a matter during the day does not amount to anything because such a dream did not come to him from the ba'al halom.[47]

Almoli, however, did not develop the issue.

The *ba'al halom* plays no role in traditional Jewish dream experience, at least insofar as one can judge from the texts. Nor is he of importance in traditional Jewish dream interpretation, despite the two references to him in the Talmud and the occasional references to him in other rabbinical works that we have noted.

Striking is the fact that when it comes to halakhic decisions, the *ba'al halom*'s decision (twice about tithing) was rejected by the rabbinic sages, as was his interpretation that a man would die on the morrow rejected on the advice of a sage. This *supernatural* dream dispenser was not considered to be an halakhic authority. Only learned sages are. Perhaps the medieval pietists who associated the *ba'al halom* with antinomianism were influenced by the Talmud's rejecting his legal decisions.

The two similar accounts of the *ba'al halom* warning about releasing a Jewish maiden and the other two similar stories of a *ba'al halom* appearing to a man whose wife's face was ugly – these four accounts in which the *ba'al halom* makes no halakhic decisions may be nothing other than contrived didactic tales in which the *ba'al halom* is only a literary device useful for teaching a moral lesson.

The *ba'al halom*, then, was of no consequence. Perhaps this was due to the first use of the term in Scripture, where it was used scornfully in reference to Joseph, the human dreamer. And a "human *ba'al halom*" never became important because there were no great dreamers in Jewish historic existence. There was, therefore, no need for either scorn or adulation.

2

DREAMS IN SEFER HASIDIM

The thirteenth century, a century concerned with dreams, witnessed the production of two major works, the *Zohar* and *Sefer Hasidim, The Book of Splendor* and *The Book of the Devout*. Both works, despite radical differences, are characterized by a high awareness of the interior life.

One of the most significant creations of the thirteenth-century Christian community, *The Romance of the Rose*, composed ultimately by two differing thinkers, Guillaume de Lorris and Jean de Meun, opens with an important observation about dreams that includes a reference to a book indicating that dreams were a subject of scholarship:

> Well might one cite Macrobius who wrote the Story
> > of the Dream of Scipio,
> And was assured that dreams are oft times
> > true . . .
> Many a dream at night
> Obscure forecasts of imminent events.[1]

Among Ashkenazic Jewry, serious attention was paid to dreams. Rabbi Moses (ben Jacob) of Coucy, whose great halakhic work the

SeMaG was finished in 1250, writes in the introduction to that work that many had asked him to write a code of Jewish law,

> and I feared composing a book available to all for I am ignorant. At the beginning of the sixth millennium [1240] there came to me a vision in a dream. "Arise, compose a book, concerning Torah, in two parts." I gave the dream much consideration. The two parts [meant] a book containing the positive commandments in one section, and a book containing the negative commandments ... Concerning the negative commandments there came to me in a dream a kind of vision saying the following, "You have forgotten the primary matter" [he had not intended to enumerate the negative commandments] ... And I attended to it [the dream] in the morning. And, behold, it is indeed a major foundation of piety. Consequently, I composed it ... And the Lord God knows that I do not falsify on the matter of the dream visions. And the Lord knows that I have mentioned them only so that Israel be strengthened in Torah and admonition.[2]

He also indicates that the "polis dream,"[3] a dream experienced by a large group of people on the same night, was an experience of both Jewish and Christian contemporaries. He says:

> In 1236 I had been in Spain to admonish [them about *mitzvot*] and God strengthened my arms through the dreams of Jews and the dreams of gentiles ... ; they [presumably only Jews] repented and a great many accepted upon themselves the obligations dealing with phylacteries, *mezuzah*, and fringes.[4]

Very early in the thirteenth century, one of the entries is the date 1203 (on the evening before Yom Kippur eve), there was produced a work in which dreams are absolutely determinative. *Responsa from Heaven*, written by R. Jacob of Marvége, is a series of legal questions that concerned R. Jacob and that he presents to the divine for answers. The present text[5] is far less than what the original seems to have been.[6] Yet what we do have may well be a representative selection. The material is essentially practical, dealing with legal questions submitted to the divine.[7] With one or two notable exceptions with which we shall deal, there is no theoretical analysis of dreams or any recording of more personal, autobiographical dreams of the dreamer.

While *Responsa from Heaven* is overwhelmingly involved with legal questions its author did evidently reflect on his presuppositions about the nature of dreams.

He entertained at least some doubt. In answer to a question dealing with purificatory ritual for all Israel so as to hasten the coming of the Messiah he wrote as follows:

> After my seeing all these [answers; he had received two] I asked: did it come into my mouth from God or not? This is how I phrased my question: Oh, Exalted King, The Great, Mighty, Awesome God, Guardian of the covenant and the *hesed* for those that love Him, Maintain Your covenant and *hesed* with us. Tell Your holy angels who have been appointed to answer dream requests, to respond to that which I will request from before the Throne of Your Glory with a true and valid answer, well ordered, with complete clarity and without any ambiguity whether it concerns a [biblical] verse or a legal decision. Here I ask [again] about all these matters which had come into my mouth in answer to the question which I raised about ritual immersion of those who have experienced nocturnal emission. Were the answers those of the Holy Spirit? Are they of any value? Is it well to reveal them . . . to the sages? Or did they come into my mouth from another spirit [the evil spirit that he prefers not to mention] and are of no value and should be hidden away?[8]

He did receive a reassuring answer. But his question is noteworthy since it raised the issue as to the criteria for validating a dream. His ultimate assurance came through a dream; in a sense, therefore, the problem remains implicity unsolved.

The only other theoretical question of R. Jacob is of particular interest since for R. Jacob it remains unsolved but for *Sefer Hasidim* it is answered with great originality. The famous statement in the Talmud, *Berakhot* 55b, "All dreams follow the mouth [of the interpreter]," was a puzzle to R. Jacob for it implied a rather arbitrary subjectivism that would invalidate the authority of the answers given in his dreams. It was so important a question for R. Jacob that it received the longest answer. His statement of both the question and the answer has a certain urgency to it:

> We were also in doubt about which it was said [*Berakhot* 56a] "Whoever gave him [the dream interpreter] a reward his dream received a good interpretation and whoever did not give a reward received a bad interpretation"; it is also said [ibid.] "Rava found a book which he [Bar Hedya, the interpreter] let fall and it was written in it 'All dreams follow the mouth [of the interpreter].' " About this we wonder and ask: Is it possible that the decrees of the Creator can be changed through the interpretation of the interpreter; is the statement to be taken literally that dreams follow the mouth of the interpreter whether [his statement] is for good or evil? Or is the matter not to be taken literally, for the decrees of the Creator are not changeable . . . ; if so why was it written "All dreams follow the mouth [of the interpreter]"?
>
> They answered: "It is so decreed [that the dreams follow the mouth of the interpreter]. Examine it; you will find [it to be so]."
>
> Again I inquired and they answered me the same. I was grieved at this. I inquired again, as I did the first time.
>
> They answered: "Indeed you know that there are people whose destiny it is that their eyes and tongues are evil; there are those whose legs are evil. And many diseases come because of the evil eye. Many die because of the evil eye . . . And at times permission is given to Satan to injure . . . Also there are people whose legs are good as it is written [Genesis 30:30] 'And the Lord blessed thee whithersoever I turned [the Hebrew *l'ragli*, which enabled him to use it for foot].' So do not wonder concerning these [dream interpreters]. For there are people whose destiny it is to be dream interpreters and their interpretation is established whether it is for good or evil. Only that it correspond to the content. Bar Hedya [the dream interpreter referred to in the Talmud] was among them. The interpretations were not established because of his merit, only because of his luck. Therefore Rava was angry at him and cursed him. And as for what was written in his book 'All dreams follow the mouth [of the interpreter]' this was not said except for people whose destiny has decreed such." So they answered me.
>
> Again I asked: If so [if luck determines all] why should one tell a dream only to one who has compassion for him.

And they answered, "a man must not invite misfortune. The one who has compassion [for the dreamer] must interpret favorably, because the angel that stands on the right [the good angel] takes the word of the interpreter, snatches it and says, 'Amen; so let it be.' And if the interpreter hates the dreamer he opens his mouth, i.e., he interprets unto evil. The angel standing on the left snatches the word and says 'Amen.' This is what determines what is done, whether for good or evil."

After a while they answered a third time: "Do not think about these words of ours, for in truth we have informed you and the secret is profound."[9]

For R. Jacob, the question as to why dreams followed the mouth of the interpreter remained unanswered. The third answer he received indicates that he did not formulate a fully satisfactory solution to his problem. As we shall see the author(s) of *Sefer Hasidim* had a very original answer to the same question.

Sefer Hasidim,[10] the product of the thirteenth-century German Jewish pietists, is an historic landmark in that it wishes to transform an entire community into a community of saints and at the same time records some of the most subtle aspects of the thirteenth-century Jewish mind that it hoped to transform. *Sefer Hasidim* has a sure grasp of everyday Jewish life, which gives it an historic rootedness along with its formulation of high-minded ideals. Its "high thinking" is anchored in "plain living." Because of this, *Sefer Hasidim* is a rich source for the student of the medieval Jewish mind.

Among the many concerns of these pietists was the dream life of their thirteenth-century contemporaries.

There is a very definite distinction in *Sefer Hasidim* between visions and dreams. One sees visions when awake. The vision may come upon a person when he first awakens, can happen in a synagogue,[11] or can come upon a person when he is taking a walk,[12] which was not preceded by sleeping. The vision is primarily involved with seeing the dead.

Undoubtedly because of this distinction, there is in *Sefer Hasidim* some conceptual similarity between visions and dreams; for dreams, too, are overwhelmingly, though certainly not completely, channels of communication between the dead and the living. There is perhaps another reason why visions and dreams have something in common. Phenomenologically speaking, all dreams can be classified as auditory, when the dreamer only hears, or visual, where the primary context is sight. *HLM* originally means "to see."[13] Certainly, biblical and talmudic dreams never lose this visual emphasis. *Sefer Hasidim* nearly always uses the verb "to see" a dream. These two common factors, that dreams and visions are by and large channels of communication between the living and the dead and that dreams and visions are both primarily visual, make for their being interrelated. Despite their association, however, they are sharply distinguished.

The best example of the interrelatedness and yet ultimate distinction can be seen in the following quotation:

> If two good friends took an oath or promised one another that if one were to die he would inform the other what it was like in that world [of the dead] either through a dream or while [the living one was] awake; if in a dream the spirit would come and whisper in the ears of the living [one], or near his brain, as the *ba'al halom* [does].[14]

Our material can be divided into theoretical observations about dreams, practical halakhic, moralistic observations about dreams, and specific records of dreams. Usually these three different elements are interwoven in a given quotation but for critical purposes it will often be necessary to impose our classificatory distinctions. The most sustained observation is the following:

> Why does the dream "come with a multitude of business" [Ecclesiastes 5:2]; and when the interpretation corresponds to the content of the dream does it follow the mouth [of the interpreter, *Berakhot* 55b]? [The answer is] nothing comes upon a man, for good or evil without first seeing in a dream some symbol [*dugma*]. No man, however, is so deserving that he should see, without ambiguities, a symbol of that which will be in the future. For thoughts are not reliable. When a man sleeps [his thoughts] mingle with the words of the angel. Therefore, they follow the mouth [of the interpreter] when the interpretation corresponds to the dream. It is said [*Berakhot* 57b] "the dream is one-sixtieth part of prophecy." It is written "And by the ministry of the prophets have I used similitudes" [Hosea 12:11]. It is written "I see the

rod of an almond tree . . . for I watch over My Word to do it" [Jeremiah 1:11–12]. Through a parable, the heart of man will understand. Therefore "And he took up his parable and said." [Numbers 24:3]; And it is written "To understand a parable [*mashal*] and a figure" [Proverbs 1:6].

In the prophetic dream the prophets' personal thoughts were not intermingled, nor were the words of the demon. In the dreams of ordinary people, however, the words of the demon are intermingled. If a man needs to evacuate he will appear very weary in his dream. If one has eaten spicy food and has drunk alcoholic beverages and has thoughts about a woman and then goes to sleep he will dream of intimacies with a woman. So, too, one whose soul yearns for God or whose soul is completely involved with some other activity will in his dream see some symbol [*dugmatan*] of that matter. All such dreams are not dreams told by the angel but come from one's thoughts, and in these one sees their symbol. Concerning them it is said "And the dreams speak falsely" [Zechariah 10:1].

But sudden dreams, when it is imagined that a woman with whom he had no previous intimacies and about whom he had no previous thoughts, and other dreams due to a demon or spirit, in these the person is not deeply asleep. It is as if his eyes were closed and he was simply thinking. For the demon does not enter into one's thoughts but whispers through the opening of the ear.

If one wishes to recognize this truth let him whisper in the morning, into the ear of the sleeper[15] something he holds dear. It will appear in the dream as if he were dreaming something somewhat similar to that which was whispered in his ear, and he will wake up. So the demon whispers and the person wishes to rise, and he [Bologna MS: the demon] becomes flatulent and cannot settle down.

These dreams come because of the demon; concerning them it is said "What has the straw to do with the wheat" [Jeremiah 23:28] for they have no value. But a dream that comes through an angel, even though one did not imagine things or speak [before going to sleep], before rising the angel comes [in the Parma text there is a lacuna; "comes" is supplied by the Bologna text] to tell him; for his thoughts and sinful fancies had already ceased. There are times at the beginning of the night or in the middle of the night when the dream is not mixed up with another dream and the man does not think about a sight he sees; for if he thinks the thought then it is not due to the angel. Neither the thought nor the dream will be established. It is similar to one who has thrown a round object which rolls to a place that the thrower has not intended.

Concerning the dreams that come through an angel it is said "I do speak with him in a dream" [Numbers 12:6]. The angel speaks through the thoughts of a man like one who leads the blind. The reason for saying "like leading the blind" is that at times he thinks the truth and at times falsehoods. So the man in his dream. Do not be surprised [at this]; even if one is awake God can turn his heart aside. Man's thoughts play him false; but all that God wants [is ultimately carried out] as it is said, "the king's heart is in the hand of the Lord as the watercourses; He turneth it whithersoever He will" [Proverbs 21:1]. [Two other biblical verses are cited to support this: 2 Chronicles 34:15 and 1 Kings 22:20.] The angel turns the thoughts into thinking about those things that God decrees. It is certainly so when one sleeps and reason does not direct the mind: For it is said "I will bless the Lord, who hath given me counsel; Yea, in the night seasons my reins instruct me" [Psalms 16:7]. It follows: at night during a dream the reins instruct. Therefore, man's reason is not [in operation] during a dream. One is like a blind man or child. There are times when one thinks about that which is true; at times, what is false. But most thoughts are not intended.[16]

A great many things in this quotation depend on the Talmud: that dreams "follow the mouth [of the interpreter]," the conception of the prophetic dream, the distinction between the dream that comes through an angel and the dream that comes through a demon, the dreams that result from eating certain foods, the dreams that result from body needs, for example, evacuation, the dreams that result from daytime fancies. There are, however, original elements, too: the statement that nothing comes upon a man, whether for good or evil, without his first seeing in a dream some examples (or similes) of what will happen, but the simile will also have its ambiguities. Original, too, is the observation that certain thoughts in dreams have their own momentum. "It is similar to one who has thrown a round object which rolls to a place that the owner has not intended."

From this lengthy quotation we may conclude that dreams are either human or supernatural in origin. Most of the observations in the quotations deal with those dreams that are primarily human in origin.

Furthermore, we must also realize that while there is here a conflation of a number of talmudic observations with some original remarks, there is no sustained, theoretical analysis of the nature and mechanics of dreams. It is a rather meandering, diffuse statement. This is characteristic of *Sefer Hasidim* as a whole; it is rich in brilliant insights that are never developed into sustained analysis, as Gershom Scholem had pointed out.[17]

Sefer Hasidim does have some other theoretical observations on dreams whose source is not supernatural:

> In a dream one is not embarrassed, for if one had [self] knowledge in his dream so as to be embarrassed it would not appear to him as if he were lying with a woman and sporting with her. For one does not do things that are embarrassing when one is awake. Dreams are [impure] fancies and a man has impure fancies and is not embarrassed by these fancies. Since no one knows what his neighbor imagines no one is embarrassed.

This first part of the quotation clearly indicates that certain dreams are the desires that are normally censored during the hours when one is awake. The observation continues: "But he who truly fears Heaven to the point of not having evil thoughts so, too, [he will have pure thoughts] in his dreams and so his dreams will appear to him."[18]

The most original observation about dreams is an analysis of a talmudic statement that is given new meaning, and which at the same time serves to justify a basic premise of these thirteenth-century pietists. The quotation begins with observations about fasting so as to avert a dream's evil consequences and then raises the question:

> If we should say "why does the dream follow the mouth [of the interpreter]," [the answer is] that if the dreams did not follow the mouth we would have to say that dreams do not come from God. And it [the Torah] follows the mouth and the interpretation. So, too, the dream which one cannot know, and whatever also comes from God, God gives one a heart in order to know and a mouth in order to interpret. If not, what is the dream's function? It is to tell us that it is a message from God, to inform us that He knows all that will come to pass in the future,

so that the human being might repent, pray, and not sin again. Furthermore they said, "there were twenty-four dream interpreters in Jerusalem
and they all gave different interpretations which were established"
[*Berakhot* 55b]. "Just as one Scriptural passage may be used for many
arguments" [*Sanhedrin* 34a]. So, too, dream interpretations. Only the
interpretation should correspond to the dream.

Similarly, the interpretation of a scriptural passage must have similarity
to the text . . . Another reason why the dream follows the mouth [of the
interpreter]: For the dream is a highly private experience and if it does
not follow the mouth [of the interpreter] it would not be possible to
repent; because it is possible to understand [the dream by virtue of its
following the interpretation], it is possible to understand its significance
for repentance.[19]

To appreciate the originality of the above quotation we must first
be aware of the fact that the Talmud never explains the observation
that dreams follow the mouth of the interpreter. Second, there are a
number of basic assumptions explicit and implicit in our quotation.
Most explicit is the notion that good dreams are a kind of prophecy and
come from God. This conception serves to connect the good dreams
with Torah, the most significant and sustained prophetic text that
comes from God. Now it is a basic assumption of traditional Judaism,
to which the thirteenth-century German pietists were loyal, that the
written Torah, which is God-given, can only be understood through
the oral Torah, originally God-given on Sinai but which rabbinic
scholars through rational analysis recover, and which ultimately serves
to interpret Scripture.

From that point of view the meaning of written Torah is determined through the oral Torah. This is the assumption of the quotation,
"Dreams follow the mouth"; as the written Torah's meaning is determined by the oral Torah, as the oral Torah is in a sense God-given, so
is the dream interpretation (i.e., following the mouth, oral) also God-
given in an ultimate sense, for it is God who has given the interpreter
a heart to understand and a mouth to interpret.

That the interpretation of dreams follows the mouth (of the
interpreter) because the dream is a kind of Torah that needs an oral
Torah enabled the thirteenth-century pietists to make sense of the

talmudic statement that in Jerusalem the twenty-four dream interpreters each interpreted differently and all became established. Their
explanation "just as one Scriptural passage can be used for many
arguments" means that dreams are a form of Scripture.

It is assumed in the tradition that the scriptural text is truly
multilevel, that it must be searched anew by each generation in order to
find new meanings that were originally implicit in the text of Scripture.
From this point of view, one passage may be used for many arguments
because it has many meanings. The meanings can be ascertained only
by systematic interpretation, which, of course, must not depart from
the intent of the text. Dreams, too, as our quotation indicated, must be
interpreted with fidelity to the original text of the dream, but like a
biblical text it is open to many arguments. So, here too, the understanding of dreams is a form of understanding a written revelation and,
therefore, can be understood through an oral interpretation. As one
interpretation cannot exhaust the true meaning of a scriptural passage
so one interpretation cannot exhaust the true meaning of a dream.

This understanding of a dream's meaning being determined by
interpretation was something that would have been of great value to R.
Jacob of Marvége, for it would have solved the problem of dreams'
subjectivism in the area of legal decisions. But R. Jacob evidently lacked
the originality of the *Sefer Hasidim* pietists.

As we have indicated, dreams in *Sefer Hasidim* are primarily visual
rather than aural. In this sense *Sefer Hasidim* maintains the original
understanding of the Hebrew root *HLM*. The verb "to see" almost
always accompanies "dream" in *Sefer Hasidim*. Even when the dream
context is communicated by voice, for example, as a dead person
speaking, the dreamer *sees* the dead. *Sefer Hasidim* has a theoretical
explanation for the visual mechanism of a dream:

> Why is a man *shown* [things] in a dream? [The dreamer] is like a man
> who comes anew among a nation whose language he does not under-
> stand; if those people should *speak* [my emphasis] to him he would not
> understand, therefore they show him through visions and likenesses
> like those who gesticulate before a deaf person who cannot hear . . . So
> they show [a person] in a dream. And one who is understanding will
> know what is being shown him, why it is relevant for him.[20]

That the dreamer is described as "a man who comes *anew* among a nation whose language he does not understand" (emphasis mine) implies that the language of dreams is a forgotten language. In order to be understood it must be communicated in symbols.

We might expect, therefore, that most recorded dreams in *Sefer Hasidim* would be rich in symbols that would need interpretation. But this is not the case. There is, on the contrary, a paucity of symbolic dreams that need interpretation. We shall look first at the observations of *Sefer Hasidim* and then offer an explanation. "He who sees a Torah scroll in an ark in his dream is being told about death."[21] The analysis is based on a convoluted exegesis of a verse in Deuteronomy: "And I turned and came down from the mount and put the tables in the ark which I had made and there they are as the Lord commanded me" (10:5). This is not the recording of a specific dream but a general rule interpreting a symbol that, we assume, occurred in dreams with some frequency. Another symbolic dream interpretation is given in the following quotation: "He who sees in a dream one preparing dough for matzot or sees a conflagration in an oven, on the morrow let him start an argument with some one and then seek [God's] mercy so that it be for the sake of Heaven and so that he sin not in contention."[22]

This, too, is a general rule that must have grown out of frequent experiences but is not here recorded as an actual case. Of these two general observations, we need say that for the medieval Jewish mind, deeply engrossed in biblical and talmudic associations, the symbolic interpretation was quite clear and uncomplicated.

We now turn to a dream, the symbolic meaning of which was immediately apparent since no exegesis is presented between the dreaming and what was done:

> It happened that a saintly sage was buried next to one who was unworthy. The saint came to all the townspeople in a dream and said, "you did me evil in that you buried me next to a toilet that has a stench. The fumes are hard on me." They placed stones between the grave of the saint and the grave of the evil-doer as a divider; from that time on he [the saint] did not come to them in a dream.[23]

The symbol was in all probability immediately clear to the people. It was a cacophonous symbol that evidently needed no interpretation.

Another symbolic dream was interpreted for the dreamer within the dream itself:

It happened to one whom they always told in a dream that he would die. Once they said to him, "Confess, he [*sic*] will die very soon." For every dream he fasted. During the dream he recited Psalm 25 and the Great Confession with much crying; and he became sick unto death. Then he saw before him something similar to a cloud in the form of a man who was carrying a great burden and in his hand was a gold coin. There was also the form of another man who, wrapped in a prayer-shawl, said "[Your] merit is that you are young and [yet] you wear the fringes that you began [wearing] once again [evidently the dreamer had repented of a temporary laxity]; the gold coin that you gave to a poor sage has redeemed you from death."[24]

This dream, too, therefore presented no problem of interpretation since the symbols were interpreted within the dream itself.

What kind of dreams, then, needed interpretation of the symbolic language since as we have seen *interpretation* is important for *Sefer Hasidim*? Interpretation by a human interpreter is, surprisingly, rare in *Sefer Hasidim*. We have only two such cases recorded:

"According [to the interpretation] of the mouth the dream follows" as is demonstrated in the case of Gideon when one interpreted his friend's dream. So, too, the following: It happened that a gentile was despondent. His friend said to him, "why do you appear so troubled?" He answered, "In my dream I saw that I was riding on a red horse which is near an unclean cow." His friend told him that he would soon die and he would be driven while on a bier. The interpreter [his friend] said to him, "if you give me a drink I shall assume the responsibility of your dream from you." He said, "on the condition that my dream will be sold to you, will I give you the drink." He [the interpreter friend] took [the condition] upon himself; he was given the drink. In two days the dream interpreter died.[25]

While the quotation ostensibly sets out to illustrate the thesis that all dreams follow the mouth of the interpreter, it gives as background of the thirteenth-century incident, the biblical story of Gideon, where two Gentiles are discussing one's dream. And the thirteenth-century incident is also involved with two Gentiles.

The second case of dream interpretation in *Sefer Hasidim* where the interpretation is not immediately apparent and is not clarified in the dream is the following: "A priest told his dream to a Jew; [the Jew] interpreted it, 'it means they will give you many churches where you will preach and teach.' "[26] We are not told what it was that the priest saw in his dream that needed interpretation, but it is certain that he saw something, and it was a Jew to whom he went for interpretation.

The two dreams that need interpretation, for the meaning is not given in the dream itself nor is it immediately clear by virtue of its own obvious significance, are dreamed by Gentiles. This is strange when we think of the serious attention paid to the issue of dream interpretation by *Sefer Hasidim.*

There is, however, a basic logic to account for what appears at first to be so contradictory. Leo Oppenheim has called attention to a characteristic of biblical dreams that has bearing for our material:

> "Symbolic" dreams are, in the Old Testament, reserved for the "gentiles." The Lord sent the Egyptian officials, the Pharaoh of the Exodus, and Nebukadnezzar, such dreams but he provided them, at the same time, with the interpreter (Joseph and Daniel, respectively) to make his message understandable.[27]

This is the case in *Sefer Hasidim.* Here the Jews also dream symbolic dreams, but the symbols are either interpreted in the dream or are immediately understandable, and they know general rules of interpretation. The dreams of Gentiles, however, need interpretation, for these are not immediately understandable nor are they interpreted within the dream itself. In our two quotations dealing with Gentiles one is an exact parallel to the dream dreamed in the Bible in connection with Gideon where a Gentile interprets the dream of his neighbor and the incident is used to teach the Jew, Gideon, something important. So, too, the dream of a Gentile interpreted by the gentile friend is quoted in *Sefer Hasidim* so a Jew can learn something. But the dream itself is a symbolic dream that needs an interpretation by the nondreamer. The other symbolic dream, dreamed by the priests and interpreted by the Gentile, is parallel to Joseph's interpreting Pharaoh's dream.

Sefer Hasidim, then, despite its stress on the symbol in dreams as a forgotten language that needs interpretation, is a thirteenth-century work remarkably faithful to the Bible's view of dreams.

What does *interpretation* mean for *Sefer Hasidim?* Of the two Hebrew verbs for interpretation of dreams, *PSHR* and *PTR, Sefer Hasidim* uses *PTR,* which occurs very few times in our text, only seven times to be exact. This is to be accounted for on the basis of what we have already said, that is, that the overwhelming proportion of dreams in *Sefer Hasidim* are immediately understandable or interpreted within the dream itself. Nevertheless, the question remains: what does it mean to have a dream interpreted either within the dream or through an interpreter? To understand "interpretation" for *Sefer Hasidim* it is necessary to understand the meaning of *PTR.* This understanding is furnished us by an analysis of the parallel Hebrew term, *PSHR,* as it is found in its Akkadian equivalent:

> The range of PSHR . . . can be . . . comprehended by "to release, remove, dispose of, relax, loosen." . . . All this forces us to assume that . . . the Akkadian *pašāru* can be used to render (a) the reporting of one's dream to another person, (b) the interpreting of an enigmatic dream by that person, and (c) the dispelling or removing of the evil consequences of such a dream by magic means.[28]

Sefer Hasidim's understanding of dream interpretation is parallel to this except that *Sefer Hasidim* rejects all magical means for removing the evil consequences of dreams. Prayers and fasting function in place of magic. But there must have been prevalent a magical view of fasting as a method of dealing with dreams, for *Sefer Hasidim* warns:

> Be sure to understand that although the sages said [*Shabbat* 11a] "fasting is fitting to a dream as fire is to flax," they mean this only when one repents together with the fast. For there was Jew who saw in a dream [presumably something evil] on the eve of the ninth of Tishri and he fasted on the ninth of Tishri and on Yom Kippur all of which amounts to two days and one night. [Yet all this fasting] was of no avail. For one is shown a harsh dream so that he might investigate his conduct. Fasting is a substitute for [animal] sacrifices. Just as a sacrifice is of no avail

without repentance . . . so too fasting about a dream [demands repentance].[29]

There are in *Sefer Hasidim*, as indicated before, dream reports that are not recorded for the establishment of the meaning of the dream. What is the purpose of reporting? Although some dreams did have specific messages, the reason for reporting the dream was deeper than simply that of imparting information. Ancient dream analysis, despite differences in time, again serves us well for our understanding of *Sefer Hasidim*:

> The message of the dream has thus to be separated from the vehicle which carries it. The vehicle in itself – that is, the dream as a means of communication between the deity and man – is fraught with awe and danger and thus has to be removed immediately whatever the content of the message be. The message of such a dream does not, once it is understood, pollute the dreaming person, whatever its content may be; only as long as it remains enigmatic is it dangerous. The interpreting is, therefore, a necessity, not performed primarily for the sake of establishing the content of the dream but intended to rid . . . the patient of the impact of the enigma. Dreams were then, as today, interpreted for therapeutic reasons.[30]

> It should, however, be stressed that this parallel is only on the surface; the "decoding" of the symbolic dream by means of psychoanalytic methods is supposed to reveal the make-up of the personality of the dreaming person as it is conditioned by his past, while the interpretation of a "symbolic" dream in Mesopotamia reveals the message of the deity addressed to the dreaming person couched in the form of a riddle and – above all – referring always to the future. All this is, of course, in absolute contrast with the modern approach to the dream experience which "analyzes" the dream content, i.e., breaks it down in the attempt to establish the motives and mechanics of the substitution – and distortion – process through which the individual psychology of the dreaming person expresses itself in the manifest dream-content. The modern expert "ana-lyzes" the dream which means, etymologically, he "dissolves" the dream; his Mesopotamian colleague "solves" the dream.[31]

> The etymology of *pašāru* fits this interpretation . . . the range of the Semitic root *pšr* can be circumscribed by the English "to solve" and its

derivatives: "to dissolve, to absolve" . . . We have *ptr* in Hebrew . . . The customary translation "to interpret" for all these verbs . . . should . . . be understood as referring exclusively to that aspect of the English word which has to do with translating. But it should be stressed that no exegetic or hermeneutic approach is involved when one speaks of the interpreting of dreams in the Ancient Near East. The symbols of the dream-language are simply "translated" into the symbols of the language spoken by the dreaming person.[32]

What was true in the ancient Near East is true of the point of view of the thirteenth-century pietists. Dream interpretation has the same meaning for them as it did for ancient Semitic precursors: "Only as long as it remains enigmatic is it dangerous. The interpreting is, therefore, a necessity, not performed primarily for the sake of establishing the content of the dream but intended to rid . . . the 'patient' of the impact of the enigma."

Therefore, according to *Sefer Hasidim*, "One should not bless an evil man . . . nor should one interpret [*ptr*] his dreams so as to say to him 'God will fulfill your requests' for there is evil in his heart."[33] Interpreting dreams rids "the patient of the impact of the enigma" by showing that dreams had desirable meanings. But ridding one of the enigma had the opposite danger, too:

> One who interprets for a Jew [that his dream means] that he will sin it is as if he caused him to sin . . . ; even though the interpreter is a sage and knows that should he not interpret [the dream so], it will be established; nevertheless, he should not interpret that the man will come into the hands of sin.[34]

To dissolve the enigma of the dream, it was at times necessary to destroy the validity of the dream. One such case in *Sefer Hasidim* is particularly valuable, for it is the only example of an *interview* about the meaning of a dream:

> A man had a dream. He came before a sage and said to him, "I dreamed that I should marry so-and-so; she said to me [after the dream] that she did not want to be married to me. I would take to wife another woman but it appeared to me [evidently, in a subsequent dream] that it would be

a sin punishable by death for I must take the one that I dreamed would be married unto me." The sage said to him, "Dreams are of no effect one way or another [*Gittin* 52a]. One cannot depend on dreams; it is not a sin for you to marry [another] woman. If it had been decreed that you marry the one about whom you dreamed she would have been amenable [to you]. If you should plan to wait many years for her to become amenable it would be both foolish and sinful for 'dreams come with a multitude of business [Ecclesiastes 5:2].' There are times when a man dreams that he must marry so-and-so because she was talked about. There are times when one dreams he must marry a woman who has actually died. Indeed, one cannot depend on dreams. After all, should one dream about marrying a married woman if he will only wait a while, then, in effect, he would be looking forward to the death of the husband. This is sinning for these are sinful thoughts. [Furthermore, while waiting] he is not carrying out the duty of propagating the human race."[35]

A number of quotations already presented indicate that the source of some dreams is an evil being. The logic of this idea, and perhaps its very origin, is clarified if we attend to ancient dream material:

These [forgotten] dreams, pleasant or evil, do not predict the future of the dreaming person nor do they warn or promise; they are but indicators of the physical and/or psychological status of the person who is experiencing them, and this status in itself is but the expression of the cultic standing of the person, in other words of the extent to which he is endowed with the protective deities who safeguard the life, success, and happiness of the individual. The natural consequence of such a concept of dreams is to see in them demonic powers, even demonic beings, who roam through the night attacking those who cannot protect themselves. This in turn is bound to give rise to . . . the Lord of Dreams, a deity who is in charge of them.[36]

After discussing the Mesopotamian demons, Oppenheim discusses a matter of particular importance for our study:

It is tempting, however, to speculate as to whether the Talmudic concept of a supernatural dispenser of dreams, the *ba'al halom* . . . reflects in any way the Mesopotamian tradition of a Dream-god. The very fact that the Palestinian version of the Talmud does not mention this angelic figure lends some weight to this theory.[37]

Dream demons and a ruler of dream demons are to be found in the dreams of the thirteenth-century Jews pictured in *Sefer Hasidim*. No doubt this was mediated by the Babylonian Talmud, a work central to their life.

Dreams are referred to as coming from God (see above, the quotations to the effect that dreams are a type of revelation), from an angel,[38] from a demon,[39] and from a *ba'al halom*.[40] The *ba'al halom* does seem to be the chief of the demons and his evil quality is indicated when it is said, "If the *ba'al halom* will tell one to transgress the mitzvot, one should not listen to him."[41] This implies that the *ba'al halom* is the great tempter, the tempter into antinomianism, untenable for traditional Judaism. The *ba'al halom* was also probably the one who was visualized in a dream report as being a man bigger in size than a house. His immense size is reiterated in the dream report, and he has a human face.[42]

Presumably, in most cases the dreamer is invaded by the dream. But the community pictured in *Sefer Hasidim* assumed that there were ways of eliciting a dream. "It happened that a *hasid* elicited a dream as to who would sit next to him in paradise. They showed him a young man who lived far away. On the morrow he prepared himself and went off in order to see him."[43] In this particular quotation we are not informed as to how one *"asks* for," that is, elicits, a dream. But we do have some evidence as to how this can be done. A *hasid*'s disciple stretched himself out on the grave of his master and requested that he be informed in a dream on the matter of ascetic practices as to whether he was being punished or rewarded. "The *hasid* came to him in a dream and said, 'come with me and I will show you.' And he brought him to paradise."[44]

It would not be wrong to infer, we believe, that the dream did not occur when the disciple was stretched out on the grave but came subsequently, probably that night, when the disciple was sleeping.

Ritual magic, a practice vigorously rejected by *Sefer Hasidim* generally, was evidently used to elicit a dream:

It happened to a man whose mother had hated him. He was not at her side when she died. She had not left a will [telling] where her money was [hidden]. The son requested of a witch that she go to work so that he might know where the money was. At night, with a knife she did what she did and then went to sleep. The demon came in a dream with the knife plunged in his heart. The son of the demon brought the man's mother and said to the witch, "Why did you plunge the knife into my father's heart." She said, "Because the man requested that you inform him where his mother's money is hidden." The demon said to the mother, "You see that the knife is in my heart until you tell me where the money is." [She explains that she refuses to do so and says] "You do not rule over me to command me after my death." . . . On the next night she said the same. So, too, the third night. The demon entreated her, saying, "I cannot bear the knife in my heart"; She said, "though it is not the law [that I must tell] and [though] I do not want to tell, nevertheless, because of your pain, I say that my money is locked well in a chest." Her son searched in a number of chests. After a few days his mother said to him in a dream, "How you have troubled me to come and inform you; many punishments will come upon you for bringing me back [from the dead]."[45]

The account concludes with the information that the money was found in a place indicated by the mother and than adds that one should not be involved with witchcraft. But it is clear, in any case, that dreams could be induced by means of witchcraft.

Another, but legitimate, way of inducing a dream is that of two friends taking an oath promising each other that the first one who died would inform the other what it was like in the world of the dead through a dream.[46] This technique depends on a prior oath that the dead person had taken while alive. But we are not told of a subsequent technique of inducing the dream to take place.

Sefer Hasidim, rich among medieval Jewish books in that it pictures all levels of Jewish society and various levels of Christian society, presents dreams of the pious sages, their disciples, and ordinary people as well, including people whose reputation was that of being wicked. There is a case of a polis dream, a dream dreamed by an entire city when a sage "came to all the townspeople" complaining that he had been buried next to an evil man whose stench disturbed him. This dream so impressed the people that they placed dividers between the graves.[47]

Ta'anit 21b has two accounts of dreams dreamed by all the people of a town.[48] But the polis dream is rare.

From the quotations we have presented in various connections, the content of the dreams is quite clear. One of the main concerns is death. There is an interest in the world of the dead, what existence is like in that world, and the place of the righteous in paradise. But there are more imperative aspects to the dreams concerning the dead. One of the recurring dreams is the question of the proper burial of the dead. We have referred above to the polis dream, in which a deceased righteous man had appeared to the townspeople complaining about being buried next to an evil man. A dream with a similar theme deserves mention: "A wicked person was buried among those who had been killed [in martyrdom]. He appeared to an important man in a dream [asking] that he be removed from among them for it was particularly difficult for them [because of his being buried among them]."[49] Presumably this request was carried out since some similar dreams were acted on:

> Concerning a man who had swallowed balsam and had died. After some years he appeared to his sons in a dream [asking] that they disinter him in order to know his difficulty. They thought that perhaps [robbers] had stripped him and he was naked; so they disinterred him and found him whole as on the day he was buried. They touched the garment in which he had been buried and it disintegrated. And he turned into dust. Why did he appear in a dream? For they found him whole . . . and [therefore] he was not fit to rest. Therefore, he appeared in a dream that [he be disintered and] disintegrate.[50]

The dead person's demand concerning his proper burial can extend even to the fastidiousness of deciding what was to be done with the lumber remnants after the coffin was made. In a case where the extra wood was used by a man for making a musical instrument the dead appeared and warned against this. The warning was not taken seriously. The instrument maker became dangerously ill. The man's son took the instrument and broke it over the grave and left the pieces there, and consequently the man was healed.[51]

Two accounts of the dead appearing are particularly noteworthy for our purposes since they furnish us with information dealing with the more subtle shadings of the medieval Jewish mind:

Many Jews were killed in troublesome times; many had decided to be killed [i.e., to choose martyrdom] and were saved. And a Jew named Israel saw in a dream a martyred one, named Sabbatai. R. Sabbatai, the martyred one, said to him, "All those that had decided to be martyred [but were saved] their portion is to be with us in Paradise.[52]

This concern is portrayed more fully in the following passage:

In one place many Jews were killed in sanctification of God's name. A small number underwent forced conversion; they did not let themselves be killed but were baptized. At night they brought the dead to the cemetery on wagons for it was far from the place where they had been killed. A martyred woman fell from a wagon [in transit] but this was not known. The dead were buried together but separated by dividers in large, wide pits. The martyred woman who had fallen from the wagon appeared to one in a dream. She was angry and said that she, too, had been martyred. He [the dreamer] investigated [and finding that the dead woman's claim was true] offered a reward for finding her. A shepherd came and showed him where she had fallen from the wagon. She was then buried with the other martyred ones. That very night she said to him, "since you gave a reward on my behalf so that I was finally buried with the martyrs, go to such and such a place where I have hidden money." It was found as she had said. There were also two who had tried to slaughter themselves but were not actually able to kill themselves. The gentiles thought they had died although actually they had not died. After some years they died. And a Jew dreamed that martyrs had said [to those two] "do not enter our domain for you, unlike us, were not killed for the sake of sanctifying God's name." They each showed the cut in the neck. "But [the martyrs said] you did not die." An old man came along and said, "since you cut yourselves in order to die [as martyrs] and you were not baptized you deserve to be with us martyrs." And he brought them in to their domain.[53]

While dreams about the dead seem generally to have been taken seriously, an incident recorded primarily to teach a lesson also implies that dreams of the dead were, on occasion at least, ignored: "A community decided to move to another place. A dead person came to one in a dream and said, 'do not forsake us, for we enjoy your visits to the cemetery. Should you forsake us, know that you will die.' They did not care; subsequently they were all killed."[54] It would be impossible to decide whether such an incident actually took place. But even if this were purely contrived in order to convince one that the dream should be taken seriously, it clearly shows that not all dreams of the dead were taken seriously by these thirteenth-century Jews.[55]

Despite the assumption that to dissolve the dream is good and the implication, more or less explicit, that a pious sage can help one to dissolve the dream, there remains the impression that dreams are essentially private affairs, and should remain so. So that "if in a dream they brought him glad tidings, or even if Elijah [appeared] or an angel, let him not tell his wife, lest she tell others – miracles are not performed in public."[56]

Unpleasant dreams, too, should be kept secret: "If a man sees in a dream either a spirit or demons let him not tell anyone. For anyone who sees demons and touches fire before telling anyone and [even then] does not tell anyone what he saw, he will not be harmed nor will he die." Nightmares, that is, spirits who come in the night to a sleeper, should be kept private.

Very little consideration is given to the times of the dream as an indication of its relevancy. The only explicit statement on the subject is "a dream that one sees at the end [of the night] will soon come about and what one sees at the beginning of the night will come about later."[58] This statement is not embedded in a larger theoretical discussion, neither is it presented to clarify any specific dreams. For all practical purposes, then, the time of dreams is not a serious consideration.

Gershom Scholem has said in describing the thirteenth-century Jewish pietists who produced *Sefer Hasidim* that their "study of Talmud was pursued with an enthusiasm which was nowhere surpassed . . . But this interest in the casuistry of the Holy Law was not paralleled by a similar gift for or devotion to speculative thought."[59]

It would not be amiss to add that their interest in the casuistry of the Holy Law was essentially pragmatic. These thirteenth-century pietists were interested in shaping a community's diurnal life. This pragmatic flair is equally evident in the dream material. While here and there are insights of high originality and great theoretical implications, the dream material in *Sefer Hasidim* is centered on the practical concern of deriving a lesson so that one might live a more pious and holy life. This is perhaps best summed up in a statement of profound poignancy:

> "all the days of the poor are evil" [Proverbs 15:15], for one must fast because of dreams. And one dreams even more than one attends to the dreams. Why are they [dreams] shown one? So that one might be troubled. And when the saintly person is troubled the world is benefited because of his merit. And he is benefited in the world to come. "In all labor there is profit [Proverbs 14:23; labor can also be translated 'trouble' or 'sorrow' and this translation in the mind of the writer(s) of *Sefer Hasidim* makes the text relevant for our quotation] and he that is of merry heart hath a continual feast" [*Ibid.*, 15:15] for he is not upset. It is good if the dreamer is not upset but is happy.[60]

This quotation is involved with a contradiction. Clearly the saintly person is shown unpleasant dreams so as to be troubled; his being troubled is a kind of vicarious atonement for the world. He is rewarded for this suffering in the world to come. Yet the same quotation concludes that one should not be troubled by his dreams.

The contradiction is clarified if we understand the assumptions of *Sefer Hasidim*. *Sefer Hasidim* generally pictures a way of life for a saint, yet it is aware of the social reality that all men will not be saints. At the same time it wishes to elevate the life of the average man, to inspire him, on the one hand, and to ameliorate his lot, on the other. So, too, our quotation talks about the saint and his dreams and the ordinary man and his dreams. The dreams of the saint cause him suffering, which is of value. The average man who must, as generally recognized in *Sefer Hasidim*, learn from his dream must also have his dream dissolved. For only through this is the even tenor of the average life possible. The basic problem is solved for both men. Dreams have their meaning. To know this is to dissolve their problematic character.

3

THE INTERPRETATION OF DREAMS *BY A* SIXTEENTH-CENTURY RABBI

Solomon Almoli's *Interpretation of Dreams,* first published in Salonika in 1515 and frequently republished in many places and times even as late as twentieth-century Warsaw, and noted by Freud in his *Interpretation of Dreams,* is without doubt the most important postbiblical, post-talmudic Jewish work of dream interpretation.[1]

Almoli, born in Salonika not later than 1486 and by 1516 residing in Constantinople, was an ordained rabbi, serving as a judge in the Jewish court and earning a living as a physician. He had composed works dealing with Hebrew grammar, and so universal were his interests that he planned an encyclopedia dealing with all of human knowledge, although he succeeded in composing and publishing only the proposal and outline.[2]

Initially Almoli's *Interpretation of Dreams* circulated in manuscript, although we are not told how this took place. He decided to publish it once he realized how helpful it was for people.[3]

Almoli had composed the *Interpretation of Dreams* because he was convinced that there was a serious gap in Jewish knowledge that he felt obliged to fill. In former times, he believed, Jews were involved with the study of dream interpretation. It was a highly developed wisdom;

there were experts in it. Its difficulties, however, caused people to neglect this study.[4] Almoli was surprised when he realized that the early sages, despite all their works, did not compose a single book dealing with dream interpretation. He found it strange that "everyone holds dreams in contempt and considers them to be meaningless."[5]

Almoli's "everyone" probably meant his learned rabbinic colleagues since he knew that his *Interpretation of Dreams* was of help to people among whom it circulated in manuscript.

Almoli was concerned that this wisdom, dream interpretation, should not disappear. He read widely[6] and composed his work. He made no claim to originality. He saw himself as a summarizer.

The decline of the wisdom of dream interpretation was due not just to the difficulties inherent in the subject and to its devaluation by the learned. This decline had been foreseen by the prophet Isaiah. The prophet had proclaimed:

> Stupefy yourselves and be stupid! Blind yourselves and be blind! Ye that are drunken but not with wine, that stagger but not with strong drink. For the Lord hath poured out upon you the spirit of deep sleep, And hath closed your eyes; The prophets, and your heads, the seers, hath He covered. And the vision of all this is become unto you as the words of a writing that is sealed which men deliver to one that is learned saying: "Read this, I pray thee," and he saith: "I cannot, for it is sealed."[7]

The loss of the wisdom of dream interpretation was ultimately God's doing. He took this knowledge away from the Jews because dreams and their meanings are a branch of prophecy. Only the pious can know this. Almoli implied that there were no pious ones in his time, which would account for the loss of this wisdom. Yet, paradoxically, his *Interpretation of Dreams* was written to revitalize this wisdom.

He deemed his book "a contribution in the hands of all because this is a time for compassion [for people]."[8] Because there are no interpreters, people can consult no one about the meaning of their dreams:

> The principal purpose of the work is to furnish the ways and true principles by which every man will know how to interpret dreams and

to understand their intent. It also brings interpretation for the details of the dream . . . what each of them indicates. It also furnishes ways and *tikkunim* to negate every evil dream and to dissolve its evil.[9]

Indeed, Almoli structured his *Interpretation of Dreams* this way. There are three sections: a section that presents the principles of interpretation, a section listing the meaning of dream symbols, and a section devoted to alleviating evil dreams.

The *Interpretation of Dreams* purports to be a book for every person. But it is implied in a number of passages that only a trained interpreter can interpret dreams: "Since the matter [of interpretation] depends on wisdom it follows that not everyone who wishes to arrogate for himself the right to interpret dreams should do so; only one among many."[10]

Despite the fact that dreams were not taken seriously by his learned contemporaries, Almoli had no doubts that dreams were of consequence. Immersed in the Jewish tradition and knowing something of the classical traditions about dreams he hoped to recover the discipline of dream interpretation for the Jewish community.

At the outset he raises the question as to why the meaning of dreams is not readily known. He suggests that four factors make the meaning of dreams so problematic: (1) they contain strange and exotic elements, since each symbol has many meanings; (2) men capable of analyzing things who can also understand the individual person (i.e., the dreamer), and related issues, are rare; (3) many meaningless things occur in a dream; (4) there can be dreams without significant meaning.

Dreams are, therefore, not easily understood. Almoli confesses that he can discuss the subject only in a very general way: "The details are forever hidden from the eyes of every interpreter." And since one can know dreams only on the basis of one's theories, "It is impossible not to make mistakes most times."[11] Almoli made no claims to omniscience or infallibility.

There are, we are told, three kinds of dreams: the highest kind is the prophetic, the lowest is the magical, divinatory dream of the false prophet, and, in between, is the ordinary dream. Almoli does not know enough, he advises his reader, to enable him to present a complete analysis of the differences between these three kinds of dreams, but he does state some differences. The prophetic dream occurs only to one who is wise, righteous, strong, and wealthy, as the sages said. It comes through an angel, according to Maimonides, but only because God so orders the angel who stands before Him. The magical, divinatory dream occurs as a result of a person's preparation in a certain way to conjure the angel. This kind of dream is "not true; nevertheless God grants them a role so that one might perceive them and recognize falsehood and thereby remove himself from that activity and shield himself from that arrogance."[12] With this observation Almoli rejected an older tradition of *Sh'elat Halom*, eliciting dreams. There were respectable precedents for eliciting dreams. Rabbi Jacob of Marvége (early thirteenth century) composed a collection of legal decisions entitled *Responsa from Heaven*,[13] for he received answers to legal problems that he had presented in dreams. He must have had some technique for presenting questions and receiving answers, although he does not mention this. The thirteenth-century *Sefer Hasidim* assumes the eliciting of dreams although it does not explain how this is done. There are occasional references in medieval Jewish works to eliciting dreams. Perhaps the most interesting is that of Moses Botarel, a Spanish Jew (late fourteenth and early fifteenth centuries). In his commentary to *Sefer Yetzirah* he gives many specific directions for eliciting dreams with the assurance that the method has been successfully tested. In all probability Almoli did not see this commentary of Botarel, since it was first published in Mantua in 1562. We can assume that Botarel's techniques for eliciting dreams used folk practices, and we can assume that Almoli knew traditions of eliciting dreams but rejected them.[14]

The prophetic dream is not a great concern for Almoli, although he does make some extended remarks about it.

The ordinary dream, the *halom pashut*, is Almoli's central interest. This ordinary, "plain" dream has its source in the divine as does the prophetic dream. But the prophetic dream is presented by the angel *who is before God*; the *halom pashut* comes simply through an angel.[15] Perhaps because of this the ordinary dream lacks the clarity of the prophetic dream, although Almoli nowhere says this explicitly. The ordinary dream, unlike the divinatory, magical dream, comes without any preparation by the sleeper. But a more important distinction between the two is that the divinatory dream comes from the "left side" through the agency of demons, while the ordinary dream comes from God through the agency of angels who serve him on the "right side." Furthermore, divinatory dreams are for the most part, or perhaps altogether, false, but there is no ordinary dream that does not contain some truth. If it does not seem to be so, we do not understand it.[16]

The ordinary dream and the prophetic dream, then, share a very important common characteristic: they are both rooted in the divine. But for a dream interpreter it is important to be aware of a crucial difference between these two types of dreams. While the prophetic dream contains no meaningless aspects and therefore does not require a parable or a riddle, nevertheless on the basis of a parable in the dream it is interpreted by the prophet. The ordinary dream, however, is not interpreted through a parable in the dream but is clarified only when it is subsequently interpreted or fulfilled.[17] The prophetic dream is interpreted within the dream itself. The ordinary dream demands a human interpreter or subsequent developments that clarify the dream's meaning.

Since the ordinary dream is actually a divine message mediated through an angel, why must such a dream occur only during sleep? Why does a person not dream when awake? Almoli's answer is:

> Dreams do not come to one while awake because the powers of the body are strong then and they press down upon the soul, but they come during sleep which is the time of the cessation of emotions and bodily powers; for "sleep is a sixtieth portion of death" and then the body does not press down upon it [the soul] as it does while one is awake.[18]

Dreams, because they are spiritual phenomena, necessitate a cessation of the physical aspects of the person. It follows, then, that the more spiritual the man the more dreams he will have or perhaps his dreams will be of greater significance. Almoli is rather insistent on this, and therefore he rejects a philosophical view which also is committed to the spiritual:

> Every man is informed [in the dream] according to his level [of spirituality]. Indeed the philosophers have written that this informing is truer for children and fools than it is for the wise, and so wrote Gersonides,

the reason being that fools and children are never tired or enervated and their senses are not troubled in acquiring things or gathering scattered impressions . . . But according to our opinion, we who believe that they [dreams] are a divine effect, the dreams of the great and wise are more valid than the dreams of children and fools. The more one is involved with intellectually cognized objects the more one will be close to God and the more fitting it will be that there should come upon him that prophetic emanation and that he should dream valid dreams.[19]

Despite the idea that dreams are spiritual and that the more spiritual the person the more valid and significant the dream, Almoli nevertheless anchors dreams in the physical:

According to the food that a man eats, so are his dreams. Coarse foods, just as they cause bad secretions in the body, so they cause coarseness in the soul . . . therefore, whoever eats them, it is certain, will not be able to receive the [divine] emanation in its fullness to the extent of one whose food is fine. . . . One must say that the more thoroughly digested the food by the time of the dream, the more valid the dream will be.[20]

Almoli never resolves this contradiction between dreams as spiritual phenomena and their being anchored in the dreamer's physical condition.

Despite occasional asides to the contrary, *Interpretation of Dreams* is a manual for the professional dream interpreter. There are, according to Almoli, two kinds of dream interpreters: the *hakham*, who knows how to interpret dreams as a result of his acquired book knowledge, and the *navon*, who has a native talent for dream interpretation.[21] The *navon* is the superior kind of interpreter, although Almoli does not say so. One must assume that *Interpretation of Dreams* is addressed to the one who learns interpretations from books, the *hakham*.

Although Almoli disagreed with the view[22] that there are dreams that have no meaning, he does maintain that there are dreams that can be caused by what a man thinks about or what one does during the day. These dreams mean nothing. This kind of dream

did not come from the *ba'al halom* but from the imagination and the power of conceptual thought . . . Therefore all the wisdom of the interpreter depends on this: that he must look into every dream and know whether it contains some intrusion which is not of the essence of the dream. After he recognizes the intrusion he must clarify and [then] make a choice as to what is the essence and what is secondary.[23]

This is, of course, no easy task. It is even complicated by an historical problem. Just as there is a difference between earlier and later generations, for the former were closer to the *Shekhinah* and were ready for prophecy in contrast to the latter who are removed, so, too, earlier dreams are truer than contemporary dreams:

> Most dreams in this era are more clogged, sealed up, and confused than the dreams of earlier times. Therefore, now greater wisdom is necessary for interpretation than was needed then. Because of this, [dreams of contemporaries] remain in darkness and there is no one to understand their intent.[24]

For Almoli, the time of dreaming is important. The day of the month on which the dream occurs makes a difference as to the meaning of the dream. Almoli lists which days portend good and which portend evil. He is of the opinion, however, that this is not a talmudic tradition but that it derives from Hai Gaon and sages after him or from an oral tradition or one based on personal experience.[25]

Every dream interpreter must know three axioms that will be of help in enabling him to interpret dreams correctly. The first axiom is that the recurrence of the same dream must be judged in terms of the nature of its recurrences. If there is no basic difference, only different hints and parables, but the sections or parts of the dreams are alike every time, then such dreams should be interpreted as having one meaning. The purpose of the change of hints and parables was not only to authenticate the dream but also to give it greater clarity. If the recurrence, however, contains differences in sections of the dream then "even though it all [seems to have] one subject matter it is fitting to interpret them as different subjects according to the number of dreams."[26]

The second axiom:

> The [interpreter's] judgment concerning the dream cannot radically break away from the content of the dream but must be involved with

matters close to him [the dreamer], concerning his soul and body or his relatives or people of his state or nation, generally what his thought and the ideas of his imagination already knew or explored, not that he [presumably, the interpreter] sees these general things in all, or most all, of their reality.

The third axiom the interpreter must know is that the dreamers do not dream what they wish to show him without changes: "The usual way is that he sees some symbol of the things they wish to show him by hint and parable."[27]

For Almoli the dream interpreter is a close student of the dreamer's *sitz-im-leben*. The interpreter has to take into consideration even the dreamer's occupation:

> It is known to every sage that although two men dream essentially the same dream the interpreter must be truly aware of the dreamer and his involvements. Their interpretation [of the two similar dreams of the two dreamers] will not be similar. Not all dreamers are equal in terms of interpretation. For example the horse at times symbolizes wisdom, at times strength. So, too, if one is a sage and a person with understanding and he sees [in his dream] a river which he is preparing to cross with difficulty and because of the strength of his horse he crosses it, it teaches [one] that because of the excellence of his wisdom he will transcend impossible or profound issues. But if he [the dreamer] is a mighty man we shall judge [the horse as representing] might. For an armed robber who dreamed that he was hung from a palm tree, the interpretation will be different from a rabbi who dreamed this. Every interpretation is according to the person's activities and occupation. The former's interpretation is for hanging; the latter [meaning is] elevation and lordship.[28]

Knowing the dreamer well, which includes knowing his occupation, accounts for the success of Joseph as interpreter. As a result of Joseph's being imprisoned with the baker and butler he knew about their respective lives; that is why he was able to interpret their dreams so correctly.[29]

The interpreter must know not only a great deal about the dreamer's life, he must also be able "to understand a parable and a figure; the words of the wise and their dark sayings,"[30] so that the hints of the dream may be determined. He must have the ability to grasp the import of the symbolic language of dreams. The understanding of ordinary language and its shifts in meaning are also important. Almoli comments on the observation made in the Talmud, *Berakhot* 56b: "If one sees a cat in his dream, if in a place where they call it *shunara*, a beautiful song will be composed for him; if in a place where they call it *shinra* he will undergo a change for the worse . . . the name [i.e., the word] is the hint, not the actual thing." Therefore, he concludes, "In these times when one sees a cat in a dream it is not to be interpreted according to the meanings given in the Talmud [in the above quotation] for the word for cat is different from the two words given in the Talmud."[31]

While one might assume that for Almoli dream interpretation is not a rigorous science like medicine or grammar but an art, dream interpretation is scientific in the sense that Almoli claimed that he had a systematic body of knowledge; but its practice depended to a great extent on the ability and flair of the interpreter, and his general cultural equipment, which served to refine that flair.

That flair was, in the nature of the case, subjective. The interpreter would have to know the dreamer, his occupation, his cultural milieu. The boundaries of this knowledge cannot, of course, be prescribed by science. But more than this was necessary. The interpreter would also have to distinguish which symbols and elements in a dream were central and which were irrelevant. This too cannot be clarified by exact science. The juxtaposition of the meanings of the various symbols in a given dream also depends on subjective flair, which is outside the realm of scientific exactitude. The interpreter must also have knowledge of language both as living personal and social speech and as an intellectual tradition. This is also not a rigorous science.

The crucial role of the interpreter is deepened and clarified if we consider another aspect of *Interpretation of Dreams*: Almoli's understanding of certain rabbinic statements. Among the most startling is the rabbinic statement that dreams follow the mouth (of the interpreter). The Talmud itself does not explain why this is so. It is illustrated by examples, but at the same time becomes more complex when it is reported that there were twenty-four dream interpreters in Jerusalem; each one interpreted dreams differently and all were established. This is even more problematic when it is said that an uninterpreted dream is like an unread letter.[32]

That dreams follow the mouth of the interpreter implies that the meaning of the dream is subjective, the subjectivity not that of the dreamer but of the interpreter. With the example of twenty-four interpreters in Jerusalem, subjectivity is so extended that one is at the brink of concluding that the dream is not important; only the interpreter is important. This would be equivalent to saying that the data are of no account for the conclusion. Conclusions are determinative. This is unacceptable for any kind of methodology. A doctor, a grammarian, or an halakhic judge, such as Almoli was, could not tolerate this methodology. Nor could a dream interpreter.

For Almoli, as for any traditionally oriented Jew, there was another problem. If God is the ultimate source of dreams, as Almoli explicitly tells us, and as Jews had also believed, then the complete subjectivity implied by the rabbinic statement is intolerable. For if a dream follows the mouth of the interpreter it is subject only to the interpreter and not to God. It is no longer a divine message. It is a human message since it is what a human being says that it is.

Rabbi Jacob of Marvége, the thirteenth-century compiler of *Responsa from Heaven*, had been involved with the problem of the dream's subjectivity. Because these halakhic responsa are dream responsa, the serious question Rabbi Jacob faced was, How could the objective validity of the decision be verified? He asked for a divine answer to be given in a dream, as to the meaning of the rabbinic dictum that dreams follow the mouth (of the interpreter). No clarifying answer was received; he never knew, therefore, whether the responsa were objectively valid or dependent on his own subjective preferences.

Sefer Hasidim, concerned with this problem, formulated an original answer to this question. Just as the written Torah depends for its true meaning on oral Torah, dreams, a kind of revelation from God, a kind of Torah, depend on an oral teaching, the oral Torah that is also divine.[33] It is highly probable that Solomon Almoli knew neither of these works for among the many relevant sources he never quotes either *Responsa from Heaven* or *Sefer Hasidim*. But Almoli did deal with this issue.

The rabbinic statement that dreams follow the mouth troubled

Almoli more than any other rabbinic statement about dreams. He gave a number of explanations without any firm conviction as to their validity. In discussing the role of food in influencing dreams he added, "Perhaps the rabbinic sages hinted at this in their saying that 'all dreams follow the mouth'; they meant that dreams follow after the food that man eats with his mouth."[34] Because it made for a too materialistic basis of dreams, a contradiction of Almoli's basic assumption of dreams being a form of prophecy, it could not be made central by Almoli.

Having stated a possible meaning, he ignores it when he later gives three possible interpretations of the rabbinic dictum that dreams follow the mouth: (1) the interpretation of dreams follow the questions and talk of the interpreter who asks the dreamer to inform him about the issues so that on their basis there might come forth a valid judgment on the interpretation; (2) every dream has many significations and even an expert cannot know them all; therefore he interprets one or two possible meanings and does not understand or concern himself about the rest. The things that the interpreter does not understand are the meaningless things; (3) the *significance* of the dream depends on its being interpreted.[35]

These three interpretations are interrelated. The first stresses the determining role of the interpreter's method and technique, that is, his questions; the second stresses the determining role of the interpreter's answer; the third simply stresses interpretation and fits in with the other rabbinic dicta. But these explanations do not resolve the problem of subjectivity.

Had Almoli devoted himself to an analysis of the implications of the first of these three interpretations he would perhaps have arrived at a methodology of dream interpretation. It was a point of view rich in possibilities.

The rabbinic statement that uninterpreted dreams are like unread letters meant, according to Almoli, that an uninterpreted dream will be fulfilled but the dreamer will not be aware of it.[36]

The rabbinic observation about twenty-four different dream interpreters each giving his interpretation and that all the interpretations were substantiated was also fraught with the possibilities of complete subjectivism. "Yet if dream interpretation is involved with wisdom and wisdom is ultimately one then," Almoli noted, "what one interpreter knows the other knows." The *Tosafot* to the rabbinic passage commented that wisdom was not involved but the sign of the zodiac (*mazal*) at the nativity of the interpreter was determinative. For Almoli,

> This does not resolve the doubt when I see that "God's word is precious" in our time, visions are not interpreted; I have not found even one who will interpret dreams so that all his words will be established. And if the matter depended on the sign of the zodiac [*mazal*] it would be fitting that now too there should be found those, all of whose words would be established, as was [the case] in antiquity . . . How was it possible that in those days there were found so many dream interpreters in one city whose luck it was that all their words were established?[37]

Almoli gives no single explicit answer to the problematics of twenty-four interpreters who give twenty-four interpretations all of which are established, but his whole approach easily solves this problem. For, as we have seen, dreams are multilevel, having various meanings. No single dream interpreter can know all the meanings. Dream interpretation is not a rigorous science but depends on the talent and flair of the interpreter. This implies various interpretations for the same dream.

Almoli's understanding of these rabbinic dicta is but an extension of his views of the centrality of the role of the interpreter.

Another rabbinic dictum – that a man is shown in a dream only what is suggested by his own thoughts[38] – was of great concern for Almoli since it implied the negation of both the spirituality of dreams and their divine quality:

> It is difficult, evil, and very bitter for me to say that the things that a man thinks about by day he dreams of by night as a hint and parable of what they wish to inform him. Therefore, I have reconsidered my ways and will change my stand to agree [with the dictum] and will say that that opinion contains two interrelated meanings: a man is informed that which will instruct [him] concerning that which he was thinking about and trying to understand; but even this they inform him only with the parables that a man thinks about by day; so the intent [of the rabbinic observation] has the general meaning that a man is shown in the dream or the interpretation nothing other than the thoughts of his heart.[39]

He proceeds to clarify this: it does not mean that what a man thinks by day and subsequently dreams about by night will be a valid dream; for Almoli has denied the relationship between the physical and the spiritual:

> But the rabbinic intent was to show us the nature and occurrence of dreams, that the things that are shown a man in a dream since they are hints and parables of what is wished to be shown to him, are always of the things that can possibly happen and actually exist as such in reality. And [consequently] his thoughts contemplate them in the day while he is awake.[40]

For Almoli, then, the rabbinic idea of a man being shown in his dreams what he thought about during the day simply means that the language of dreams, forms, and symbolism derive from diurnal experience; this is all that a man knows and consequently it is only through these channels that he can learn. But the content of the dream is divine and it is not caused by man's diurnal thoughts. This assumption is extended by Almoli to clarify what was otherwise an enigmatic rabbinic observation: "Because dreams are a divine affluence the rabbis said 'he who sleeps three days without a dream is called an evil man': the reason [for the rabbinic statement] is that it is apparent that the man is not ready for prophecy."[41] Since the ordinary dream, which is the central concern for the *Interpretation of Dreams,* is prophetic to the extent that it is a divine revelation, one who does not dream is clearly not fit to receive God's word. Lack of dreams, therefore, is an indication of bad character. But the evil man is not completely lost. In commenting on Rabbi Johanan's statement[42] that "three kinds of dreams are fulfilled" among which is "the dream which a friend has about one," Almoli says that because the person was not fit to receive the divine afflatus it was given to another for him.[43] This observation does fit in with Almoli's general view of the ordinary dream being a kind of prophecy. Just as the biblical prophets were recipients of God's word that was brought to a sinning community, so too one can dream about and for one's friend, a friend who is too evil to receive God's word in a dream. What the biblical prophet is to the sinning community the dream is to his friend – a messenger.

Another comment on a rabbinic dictum is worth noting:

> And that which they said in the Gemara "only if the interpretation
> corresponds to the content of the dream" meant that the interpretation
> should be in accord with the dream and should teach [that] which the
> *ba'al ha-halom* hinted at. For if [the interpreter] interpreted that which was
> appointed to him [the dreamer] not in a true way there is no doubt that
> it [the dream] will not be established.[44]

The problem of the divine objective meanings of the dream and
the interpreter's subjectivity is never truly resolved.

The dream interpreter is, of course, central for dream interpretation. But his role depends on a dreamer. While we have mentioned the
dreamer before, there are some other considerations that must be made
explicit. Almoli's admonishment is particularly interesting:

> A man must guard and remember all the things of his dreams; he must
> examine them minutely and care for them. For according to his care so
> they inform him. If they see that he does not care for them and does not
> consider them they do not inform him of major things but of insignifi-
> cant and irrelevant things. After one cares for them and understands
> their interpretation let him strive to carry out their words . . . Because
> this striving is necessary in the matter of every dream and without it the
> dream is practically nothing.

The man's reaction to his dream, then, has a twofold importance: the
heavenly powers will continue to give him dreams; and he will,
knowing the interpretations as a result of his attentiveness, strive to
carry out the meaning of his dreams. But Almoli added to this observation the following:

> Therefore, Joseph was obliged to give counsel to Pharaoh . . . for this
> affects every genuine interpreter, to the extent that his interpretation
> will be established. If he does not do this [give counsel], it [his interpre-
> tation] will not be established and it will not be known that he
> interpreted truly.[45]

This added function is never explored by Almoli; had he done so his book would have dealt with therapy and would have perhaps been a profound work.

What is the "striving" that the dreamer engages in? Presumably the wise counselor outlines a course of action for the dreamer so that he should do what the dream suggests should be done. The question, therefore, is, Since there are evil dreams that will be established, because the interpreter cannot change dreams from bad to good and his counsel cannot be that of bypassing the evil dreams, for dreams are, after all, divine messages, why should one go to a dream interpreter when one has what seems to be an obviously evil dream?

Furthermore, when it is apparent to the interpreter that it is an evil dream why should the dreamer be told? This had been raised by Almoli:

> This is a relevent question, since the interpreter lacks the power to change [the meaning of the dream] in favor of the dreamer and in any case the message of an evil dream will be established, of what value is the interpretation? It would be better [for the interpreter] to keep quiet and not let him [the dreamer] know the evil tidings which [if told] present him with two evils: worry about the future and the very establishment of the dream. If the interpreter is silent [about the evil meanings] it presents him with one evil, the establishment of the dream. But not the worry.[46]

Almoli insists, however, that the interpreter tell the truth no matter how unpleasant the truth is. For if it is an evil dream the dreamer can pray to God, who can do what no one else can, namely, reverse the dream from evil to good. This constitutes man's striving: if it is a good dream he should strive to carry it out, though why this is necessary Almoli does not say. If it is evil he should strive to keep it away, and also pray for divine mercy.[47]

Embedded in a long discussion on the time span for dream fulfillment he observes:

> As for the *zaddik* they inform him [long in advance] that which they wish to have him know so that he will have the leisure to strive to

achieve the interpretation. Therefore, his dreams are delayed in terms of fulfillment. But for the evil person, it is not worthwhile to let him know in advance. Only when the matter is nigh so that he will not have the leisure to strive [does he have the dream]. Therefore, his dreams are quickly fulfilled.[48]

Part 2 of *Interpretation of Dreams* contains twenty-five pages devoted to the meaning of dream symbols, arranged according to five different categories:

1. Inanimate things, namely, land, places, seas, rain, fire, snow, wind, and so forth.
2. Flora, namely, trees, plants, boats (because they are made of wood), and the products that come from these things.
3. Fauna, namely, cattle, wild animals, fish, birds, and their products such as milk, honey, cheese, cooked foods made from meat.
4. Human beings, namely, men, kings and princes, women, lying with women, the deceased.
5. Heavenly things, namely, constellations, thunder, clouds, rain, and so forth, and the Divine Torah, which is from heaven.

These five categories are, in turn, organized into sections. The range of objects is most extensive; hundreds of objects and their respective meanings are listed. This material became perhaps the most popular part of the *Interpretation of Dreams*, being reprinted with quite some frequency without attribution. Jacob Emden, for instance, included only this part in his edition of the traditional *Order of Prayers* first published in 1745 to 1748, reprinted by him, and reprinted twice even as late as the twentieth century. Almoli himself must have considered this part of his book of particular importance because he continually cites the sources of his knowledge in this part more than in the other parts of the book. For these sources he does not refer to any thinkers, Jewish or gentile, that he otherwise quotes. His sources here were the *Zohar*, dream books popularly attributed to Rashi, Hai Gaon, Yoseph

Ha-Zaddik, and Daniel, as well as books of the gentile nations, anon-ymous books, and the dream symbols of the Talmud.

Most of the symbolic meanings are given apodictically, but some are explained as being what they are by virtue of association with biblical verses because of an actual word or assonance between two different words.

Almoli was rather sophisticated about the use of these lists of dream symbols. He wrote:

> It is impossible for all the very detailed things that a man might possibly see in a dream to be remembered. These are but chapter headings and clarifications only, on the basis of which the interpreter can juxtapose and interpret what will have been seen. It is something well known that it is not fitting to interpret all the details of the interpretations so [i.e., in the same way] always. But everything [should be interpreted] in accord with the place, the time, and the condition in which the dreamer is [situated]. And [also to be considered] is the connection of the matters which will come around the [dream] vision. Everything [should be interpreted] in accord with the criteria and standards that we clarified in the [previous] sections. Furthermore it should be known that all the interpretations that we referred to as the interpretation [*sic*] of the simple things that it is possible for one to see in a dream.
>
> But he must yet examine and add on the basis of his own knowledge and must understand all the combinations that enter into a dream. It is right to do this in order to understand the general themes [*K'lalot*] of the dream; for in any dream that occurs one must first note all the particular things in it, what does each of them written in this book indicate. As for those of them not written down [in this book] let one judge by those written down or by his own estimates. When he knows what each one indicates let him estimate and look into it with his knowledge and intellect in order to harmonize the [different] parts, to interpret them so as to indicate one matter or event. Let this be [done] after one has set aside all the meaningless things in the dream.[49]

Part 3 has three divisions: Rules Concerning Fasting on Account of an Evil Dream, Rules Concerning Dream Amelioration, and Rules Concerning Untying the Dream.

There was, and perhaps still is, the practice of fasting on account of an evil dream. In five chapters of some ten pages, Almoli discussed this subject quoting the talmudic material, not particularly extensive, and also the posttalmudic rabbis. The Talmud's suggestion that one fast to avert the message of an evil dream led to a serious question: How soon should one fast after having suffered an evil dream? This, in turn, became problematic if on Friday night one had the evil dream. Should one fast on Saturday even though fasting on the Sabbath is prohibited?

The medieval authorities discussed this question, knowing the oft-quoted apothegm, "Fasting is as potent against a dream as fire against flax."[50]

Almoli quotes many authorities on the issue of fasting on the Sabbath to avert the message of the evil dream. There were different views on the matter. Almoli's interpretation stressed the *psychological* value of dealing promptly with the problem. "It is fitting," he wrote, "for one to strive and save [oneself] from all evil mishaps that break forth against one, while one is still hot [and bothered]. It is not meet to leave the matter to cool down. For then one will not be able to extinguish the blaze."[51] Almoli validates his insistence on promptness by quoting the Scroll of Esther that has Mordecai warning Esther, "For if thou altogether holdest thy peace at this time then will relief and deliverance arise to the Jews from another place" (4:14). *This time* is significant for Almoli. It means "promptly."

The psychological and biblical validations of prompt action serve as Almoli's introduction to the question of fasting on the Sabbath to avert the message of an evil dream. Quoting a number of rabbis' opinion that "in this era one must not 'fast about a dream' on the Sabbath because we are not expert at interpretation of dreams, to know which [dream] is good and which is evil," he nevertheless opts for folk practice: "The whole [Jewish] world has already been accustomed to fast even on the Sabbath [to avert] three particular dreams: upon seeing [in a dream] a burning Torah Scroll, The Day of Atonement during *Neilah Time* [i.e., the awesome Closing Prayer], the beams of one's house or one's teeth falling." And, Almoli added, that he has, however, found in a book that one fasts only about *these* dreams even on a Sabbath but not about other dreams: "In a[nother] book I found that there are four dreams about which one who sees them must fast; and Sabbath was not mentioned, namely, one who sees the Day of

Atonement, and *Neilah* was not mentioned, and the reading of the Torah and marrying a woman [traditionally a fast day] and one whose tooth is falling out." In the unnamed second book Almoli also read, " 'He who sees a dream and is worried about it' [*Berakhot* 55b] let him do one of three things: fast or give charity or have it ameliorated before three friends."[52]

Reflecting on the folk practice that he recorded and the observations he read in the two books he concluded that "since nothing at all of this [restriction of fasting about dreams on Sabbath] is mentioned in any book that one can rely on, it is meet to fast about any evil dream that will appear to us, even on the Sabbath."[53]

Two other problems about fasting about evil dreams were discussed by Almoli. The first concerned reciting the prayer "Answer us, O Lord, answer us on the day of our fast," a prayer recited on *public* fast days. Almoli was of the opinion that an *individual* does recite this prayer if *he* is fasting on account of an evil dream. But it is to be recited at a point different from the usual one, during the Prayer of the Eighteen Benedictions.[54]

The second question about this fasting is resolved in a few words with a hint of a kabbalistic, esoteric interpretation: one should fast in atonement for having fasted on a Sabbath to avert an evil dream.[55]

In this third part of *Interpretation of Dreams*, Almoli discussed the Amelioration of Dreams[56] prayer service and the prayer about dreams recited when the priests bless the congregation during the holiday services.

Almoli transcribed the Amelioration text, referring to the posttalmudic additions, and discussed suggested variant readings, which he rejected. He analyzed the "intention" of this prayer and went on to "answer difficulties and questions" about it, for example, why three men and not ten men, the number for a quorum, join the man who had the anxiety dream. Raising eight questions, mostly about the formulae of the service, Almoli proceeded with a rather prolix discussion about the evils that trouble humanity. He does this in order to demonstrate that the Amelioration prayer deals with these evils. His analysis strikes one as belabored and artificial.

The section on the prayer about dreams during the Priestly Benediction is brief. Almoli transcribed the prayer with the added note that its purpose was the amelioration of the *forgotten* dream in contrast to the remembered dream of the Amelioration service. He also noted that while it would seem that the Talmud prohibited the recitation of the dream prayer when the Priestly Benediction was recited on a Sabbath, "the people [*ha-olam*] is accustomed to recite it even when the priests do not recite the blessing [before the congregation] and only the precentor recites it" as he repeats the Eighteen Benedictions. For Almoli, "The rule is with them," that is, the practice of the people is valid. And Almoli added, "I say that it [the prayer about dreams] should be recited [during the Priestly Benediction] even on the Sabbath . . . I have come in this book to establish the custom of the Jews who recite this prayer even on the Sabbath."[57]

The last subject discussed by Almoli (omitted in the Warsaw 1902 edition, quite understandably, since by the twentieth century it was irrelevant) was "untying," that is, declaring permitted, the dream. This rubric referred to what seems to have been a recurring phenomenon in traditional Jewish communities. A person dreamt that a ban had been imposed upon him; a person dreamt that he had made a vow or taken an oath in a dream.

The locus classicus is the talmudic tractate *Nedarim*: "Rabbi Joseph said: If one was placed under a ban in a dream ten persons are necessary for lifting the ban." Rabbi Joseph discussed the academic qualifications of these ten and the possibility of substitute, less qualified, persons. And two rabbis, in this text, discuss the possibility of the ban being lifted by the one who, in the dream, "had imposed it."[58] Almoli transcribes the whole text, including parts I have omitted, and its last sentence: "Just as grain is impossible without straw – so there is no dream without meaningless matter." He also presents the opinions of the later authorities to the effect that one who dreams of being placed under a ban must be freed from it by a convocation of ten men.

As to the person who in a dream takes an oath or a vow, Almoli mentions different opinions by a few authorities and quotes the decision of the great Rabbi Asher ben Jehiel (1250–1327) that oaths or vows made in a dream "are nothing and are not in need of a request" for absolution.[59]

For us, influenced by Freud's view that dream interpretation reveals the personality of the dreamer, it would be well to reflect on what Almoli means by "interpretation." It is clear that dreams do not reveal the dreamer. Dreams reveal the divine word.

Oppenheim, as discussed in chapter 2, "Dreams in *Sefer Hasidim*," analyzed the terminology and meaning of dreams and dream interpretation in the ancient Near East. Almoli's *Interpretation of Dreams* shows remarkable continuity with the ancient views. That "the Akkadian pašāru can be used to render (a) the reporting of one's dream to another person, (b) the interpreting of an enigmatic dream by that person, and (c) the dispelling or removing of the evil consequences of such a dream by magic means"–these three meanings of pašāru,[60] which is the cognate of Hebrew *PTR* actually serve as the very structure of Almoli's book, which as we noted has three sections. The first section is primarily involved with dream reporting, for it discusses not only why dreams should be remembered and reported, but also an analysis of that "other person" to whom one reports his dream. The second section contains the index tables used in interpreting the enigma. The third section contains the religious laws about dreams, including prayer and fasting so as to avert the evil consequences of dreams. It is the third meaning of pašāru–the dispelling or removing of the evil consequences of such a dream by magic means. Of course, fasting and prayer, and other practices mentioned in this section, are not magic means. But in the sense that prayer and fasting are techniques and are involved with the supernatural we see that the third part of Almoli's book is parallel to the third rendering of pašāru.

As in the ancient Near East, "the message of the dream is to be separated from the vehicle that carries it"[61] is also Almoli's assumption. The interpreter knowing *mashal* and *melitzah* (a proverb and a figure) and knowing the life of the dreamer has the task of separating the message of the dream from the symbols that carry it: "The vehicle in itself, the dream as a means of communication between the deity and man, is fraught with awe and danger and thus has to be removed immediately whatever the content of the message be"; this is implied throughout Almoli's work but made explicit near the beginning when he explains why he calls it *mᵉfasher halmin*, interpretation of dreams, so that everyone will be able to interpret his or her dreams.[62]

Almoli's explanation of the title of his book is practically a summing up of Oppenheim's analysis of the Akkadian pašāru but of immediate interest are the last two verses: *lᵉvatel* every dream and

l^efasher its evil; for these are really equivalent; here therefore *l^efasher*
means *l^evatel*, or as Oppenheim states it, the "vehicle . . . has to be
removed immediately whatever the content of the message be."[63]

It is remarkable that a sixteenth-century European Jew main-
tained ancient Semitic categories of thought.

Yet this judgment must be tempered.

Almoli is aware throughout his book of the dreamer, his language, his occupation, "matters close to him, concerning his soul and
body, or his relatives or people of his state or nation." As we have
indicated previously, crucial for Almoli is the *sitz-im-leben* of the
dreamer. Almoli's distinction between a robber dreaming he was hung
from a tree and a rabbi dreaming the same is a good example of this.
Throughout the first section of the book, the emphasis is on the
dreamer's personal life. Almoli is at the very brink of breaking with
ancient modes of thought. He is at the threshold of the modern view
where the interest in dreams is no longer the divine source but rather
man the dreamer and the practical concern for therapy. Had Almoli
pushed his premises to their limits his view would have been radically
reoriented. Yet this judgment, too, must be counterbalanced by another
consideration.

We have noted Almoli's observation:

> While the prophetic dream contains no meaningless things and there-
> fore does not require a parable or riddle; nevertheless, on the basis of
> parable [in the dream] it is interpreted; the ordinary dream, however, is
> not interpreted through a parable in the dream but is clarified, for it does
> have meaningless elements, only when it is interpreted or when it is
> fulfilled.[64]

As pointed out before, this means that the prophetic dream is interpreted within the dream itself; the ordinary dream demands a human
interpreter (or subsequent developments).

The significance of this is apparent if we reflect on biblical
dreams. Oppenheim has pointed out that " 'symbolic dreams' are, in
the Old Testament, reserved for the 'gentiles.' " He also adds "to his
own people the Lord speaks in 'message'-dreams and not in 'dark
speeches.' "[65] In the Bible, then, dreams to Israelites, for example, the

Joseph dreams, are immediately clear or are interpreted within the dream; only dreams to Gentiles need an interpreter.

Here is where Almoli apparently evinces a break with biblical views of dreams. For Almoli, dreams to Jews also need an interpreter. Yet this is not a break with the Bible. For as we have seen, Almoli believed that the Bible predicted the attenuation of prophecy and the interpretive skills of the Jews. Undoubtedly something else is involved here.

Chapter *Ha-Ro'eh* of tractate *Berakhot*, the locus classicus of rabbinic views of dreams, which was very important for Almoli, assumed, in contrast to the Bible, that an interpreter is crucial for Jewish dreams. A point of view different from the Bible's in a work so profoundly committed to the Bible is rooted in a larger consideration. The rabbinic tradition asserted that prophecy had ceased with the prophetic ministry of Haggai, Zechariah, and Malachi. While there was what might be called a glimmer of prophecy through the *bat kol* or Elijah's visit, prophecy had disappeared and "a wise man is even superior to a prophet" (*Baba Batra* 12a). It would follow, then, that dreams were not what they had been in biblical times. As prophecy was radically attenuated, the dream as divine revelation had become radically attenuated. It had become what Almoli in the sixteenth century was to call the "ordinary dream," not without anchorage in the divine, but essentially involved with the socioeconomic-cultural rootedness of the dreamer. As it was not a prophetic dream in source of origin, so too it was not a prophetic dream in terms of the recipient; therefore, it needed a sage or technical expert to make sense of it.

Almoli's views are controlled by these assumptions. It is not a secular view of dreams that brings Almoli to concentrate on the dreamer and his *sitz-im-leben*. It is the rabbinic notion that prophecy has for all practical purposes ceased. They do not, therefore, have the immediate clarity of biblical dreams. Interpreters are needed. That Haggai, Zechariah, and Malachi are the last of the prophets in the Bible, and that there are passages in the Bible that indicate that prophecy will sometimes cease would lead one to assume that it is not only a rabbinic but also a biblical view that prophecy ceased at a specific time. In this sense it might be said that Almoli's break with the biblical view is not a break but an affirmation. The difference between the two views is significant but presupposes the affirmation of the same set of assumptions. All that is different is the historic situation.

Almoli, as previously indicated, had read widely. He was at home in the vast rabbinic legal and aggadic literature. He was also well read in rabbinic philosophical works such as Maimonides' *Guide* and Gersonides' *Wars of the Lord*. A work which he quoted with quite some frequency was the *Zohar*, the classic Jewish mystical treatise, which Almoli called *Midrash Zohar* and, at times, *Sefer Zohar*. Evidently it was not quite "canonical" yet, at least for him; but he must have taken it at face value, as tannaitic, for he saw himself in the tradition of Kabbalah. Although this was not said explicitly, he indicated this en passant in his introduction to the section on dream symbols when he noted that the interpretations are based "on the way of Kabbalah." To this he added:

> The sages of the Talmud were great sages and kabbalists; so, too, Rabbenu Hai [Gaon] was a very great kabbalist and by virtue of his wisdom in Kabbalah he wrote these [dream] interpretations. And so, too, all the rest of the sages and prophets, they were all kabbalists; by means of the wisdom of the Kabbalah they elicited these interpretations. And I had already found my strength in this matter in the *Midrash ha-Zohar*.[66]

This reference to Kabbalah, his hint of the esoteric near the conclusion of the *Interpretation of Dreams*,[67] and his quotations from the *Zohar* are evidence of his kabbalistic orientation. That he was not more explicit about his Kabbalism was not because of disingenuousness. He had written not a kabbalistic treatise but a handbook on dreams, a Jewish handbook on dreams.

It was composed for a Jewish reader, one who knew biblical and rabbinic Hebrew, could understand the classical Jewish sources, and who was committed to the truth, that is, the validity, of these sources. Almoli had, of course, read works of gentile thinkers;[68] but they were not of great importance for his understanding of dreams.

Almoli's *Interpretation of Dreams*, of major importance historically in the Jewish community, was no more than a handbook. It was not a work devoted to an exploration of the nature and function of dreams.

Almoli's a priori assumption is that dreams, even the ordinary (*pashut*) dream, are of divine origin. He knows this not by means of analysis but by accepting the biblical-talmudic-medieval Jewish tradition. He did not study dreams; he studied a tradition, or perhaps one should say "traditions," about dreams. He then composed a handbook that would serve, he hoped, to reestablish the discipline of dream interpretation in the Jewish community and that could serve people who were troubled by their dreams.

This *Interpretation of Dreams* is a kind of readers' digest of the Jewish tradition of dream interpretation and therapy. Its goal was not the development of a systematic, "scientific" theory of dreams. Almoli did not, for example, formulate a critical vocabulary for understanding the nature of dreams, for example, "manifest content" and "latent content" of Freud's vocabulary. Nor did Almoli discover anything like "an empirical method for interpreting a dream [that] involves free association,"[69] which Freud developed.

These, however, were not his concerns. In the very second paragraph of his *Interpretation of Dreams* Almoli wrote:

> There was the custom and habit in early times of men becoming recluses and being involved with this wisdom [of dream interpretation], and its ancillaries, in order that any one who dreamed a dream might come to him [*sic*] who would tell him [the dreamer] the true intent of the dream. And this knowledge would not be useless.[70]

Almoli did not succeed in reestablishing the discipline of dream interpretation in the traditional curriculum of synagogue and yeshivah (Talmud academy) but his *Interpretation of Dreams* was widely read because it was frequently reprinted at least in part and, at times, in toto even in the twentieth century.[71]

4

AN IRAQI JEWISH DREAM
INTERPRETER

Dream interpretation was available in at least one Jewish community as recently as the late nineteenth and early twentieth centuries.
We know of one traditional Jew who served people in his community
as a dream interpreter, although he did this in no official capacity.

Judah Ftayya (1859–1942) lived most of his life in his native city,
Baghdad, Iraq. He was a learned talmudist and a kabbalist. He wrote a
number of books, including a commentary on Vital's *Tree of Life*, and a
work entitled *Minhat Yehudah*, a collection of comments, some brief
and some rather extensive, on selected verses of the Bible. In this work,
first published in Baghdad in 1933, he recorded his interpretations of
the dreams of people who came to him for interpretation and also
recorded his own dreams.[1]

In his introduction to this collection of biblical comments he
notes that "there will be clarified, at times, the matter of dreams and
their interpretation in order that thereby a person will be able to
recognize and test that [*sic*] dream whether it came by means of an
angel or by means of demons and harmful spirits." And Ftayya adds
that a person, therefore, "will be able to understand and interpret that

dream without the necessity of asking those who are expert at dream interpretation."[2]

There were, then, it is implied, men in Iraq who were Ftayya's contemporaries and who were "professional" dream interpreters. Ftayya's book, along with its biblical interpretations, was to serve as a self-help manual for people to enable them to interpret their dreams without consulting a dream interpreter.

Ftayya distinguishes between the "true" dream that comes by means of an angel and the one that comes through a demon. During the "true" dream, the dreamer's "spirit is not troubled during sleep while seeing the dream but only when he awakens . . . The rule here is that the dream that comes by means of an angel will be well arranged, not mixed up because of matters unrelated to one another." The dream that is caused by demons, however, frightens the dreamer, "makes him anxious, piles up unrelated matters . . . his heart pounds and he wakes up because of great fears." And, Ftayya suggested that to deal with this type of dream, one "should recite the She'ma or say 'Impure [one], impure [one], run away from here.' "[3]

The demonic dream was of concern for him and his contemporaries; for he discusses, at some length, how the demons act. They whisper in the dreamer's ear; they play around with him in order to make him anxious; they take erotic advantage of the dreamer. The demons know what excites human beings.

The person who has had such a dream must realize that even if he fasts or does penance to ameliorate such dreams "and does not ask of a sage who knows the difference between a dream that comes through an angel and the dream that comes through a demon, let him know that he is destined for more difficult, evil, and bitter dreams."[4]

These demons were gentile demons. But there were also Jewish demons. They have one distinctive characteristic: "They make themselves out to be like the early prophets and *tannaim*. There are among them those who make themselves out to be like the judges and the well known sages who passed away . . . At times they say that they are Abraham, Isaac and Jacob."[5]

These Jewish demons are careful not to make the dreamer anxious, encouraging one to perform pious deeds: studying *Zohar* and the Book of Psalms and performing midnight vigils. They force upon the person ablutions and ascetic practices to the degree that he is close to becoming sick or mad.

Ftayya discusses these demons at length and adds that "many times people brought sons and daughters to me because they saw visions."[6] He is so busy, however, that he can give his reader only one instance of a visit by a demon.[7]

In the year 1911, during the month of *Tammuz*, an 11-year-old boy was brought to Ftayya who claimed that Elijah talked to him whenever the boy called for him, the only condition being that the boy be alone. Ftayya was skeptical of this Elijah, although two fellow sages were convinced of the truth of the claim. Ftayya persuaded the lad to test this Elijah by asking the demon to translate into Arabic a verse in Jeremiah: "Thus shall ye say to them, 'the gods that have not made the heaven and the earth, these shall perish from the earth, and from under the heavens' " (10:11). Demons were uncomfortable with this biblical verse, as Ftayya well knew, because it disparaged them; they did not want to translate. And so it happened. This "Elijah" was a demon; he begged off and ran away.

With the introduction about demons and their "false" dreams and visions, Ftayya next discusses "true" dreams. He classifies true dreams according to the hint (*remez*) given in dreams: the hint that indicates what will occur in the distant future, the hint that intimates a man's particular sin, and the one that concerns the husband and wife relationship.

Of the first type, dreams about the future, he refers to those of the three biblical figures: Joseph, Nebuchadnezzar, and Daniel.

Of the second, the *remez* of a man's particular sin, the examples he presents are those of cases with which he dealt. A man asked for Ftayya's interpretation of a dream in which he had placed his hand phylactery on his head and the head phylactery on his hand. Ftayya gives the interpretation, "I said to him that he had anal intercourse with his wife and since his was a great soul he was being rebuked for this in order that he be admonished and be on his guard from now on."[8] Ftayya does not record the reason for this interpretation.

He gives two other examples of this type of true dream. His interpretation of a thrice-recurring dream of worms coming out of a man's left thigh was that the man "had intercourse with an Arab woman three times; therefore he was shown worms in his thigh because it was the beginning of his sin as it is written, 'When the Lord doth make thy thigh to fall and thy belly to swell.' "[9] Another example is that of a man whose wife "talked with all kinds of men, Jew and gentile, and she was a loose woman." The husband dreamed that his wife was the wife of a high priest. Ftayya recorded, "I said to them," evidently they both came to him for the interpretation, "that she had committed adultery." He added that he never did hear from them whether or not his interpretation of the dream was valid.[10]

For two of the three examples of the dream that hint at a man's sin he does not explain to the reader of his book, and presumably not to his client, why he interpreted as he did. Nor did he record any analysis of the difference between this second type and the third type, the one concerning husband and wife, although both share a common theme—sexuality.

The examples given of the third type of dream are similar to each other. One concerns an adult *yeshivah* student who studied all night in a different institution each night of the week, except on Friday night, when he returned home. By then he was so exhausted that he would fall into a very deep sleep. One Friday night, he dreamed that a man appeared to him, saying, "A *tzaddik* should come to his table." The student did not know the meaning of this dream. The man in the dream returned (we are not informed whether it was on the same Friday night) and said, *"Hen, hen* [the Hebrew word for *grace* with the kabbalistic connotation of esoteric wisdom] for the man who understands."

Immediately the student understood that the dream's message was his neglecting the Friday-night conjugal duty.[11] Since the student interpreted his dream without consulting anyone, he must have reported it to Ftayya, presumably because Ftayya was known to be a "professional" dream interpreter.

Ftayya notes another instance of this type of true dream—the husband–wife relationship. In Baghdad on a Friday night a sage dreamed that he was studying with his sons on the eve of the Feast of Weeks and that he placed nine wicks in three clay pots. He poured in sesame oil, lit the wicks, and wondered why he placed the wicks in those containers rather than in glass lanterns. During this dream the sage was aware of the fact that as long as the burning wicks remained high they illuminated the walls of the room; as they burned down they lit up only what was immediately above them. Then the sage awoke, fearful about his three sons, for a fourth had died some time ago. Concerned about the dream's meaning, he fasted the rest of that Sabbath in order to avert the possible evil portent of the dream. Later that afternoon he happened to meet Ftayya and recounted the dream. Ftayya gave the man "a simple interpretation" (unrecorded), unsatisfying to the man, who finally persuaded Ftayya to tell him "the true interpretation." The "true" meaning was that the sage had arisen from his sleep three times to fulfill the commandment of conjugal duty but each time abstained and "therefore they showed you this dream."[12]

The sage confirmed Ftayya's account of what had transpired the previous night and accepted the interpretation of the dream. But he wanted to know what *remez* in the dream served as the clue for the interpretation. Ftayya explained that "the three wicks were the three flames of love that are drawn from the two limbs and [from] the *Tzaddik* [here a kabbalistic connotation of *phalos*] and yet lit them three times. But they were in an earthen vessel and did not illuminate properly. They were as if extinguished."[13]

Ftayya also told the sage a rule of dream interpretation, one of the very few rules of dream interpretation formulated in this work:

> Let this rule be at hand: Most of the dreams that come through an angel are clarified by the esoteric [i.e., kabbalistic] tradition. Because the angel is spiritual therefore they [*sic*] make the *remez* according to their way; particularly in such matters as that between husband and wife they show a person a great *remez*. And because they were concerned about your not having fulfilled the commandment of conjugal duty they showed you the dream.[14]

Ftayya recorded other dreams that he interpreted. A woman who was a miller requested him to interpret her dream. One morning while grinding grain she found a date that she ate after reciting a benediction, returned to work, and then fell asleep. She dreamed of an old man who commended and thanked her for saving him from his troubles, although her deed was only of partial help. Ftayya explained to her that in the date was the reincarnated soul of the old man. Through the woman's eating that date the man rose up two degrees from the level of plant life to the level of a human being. This was achieved by the woman's reciting a blessing upon eating the date; but she had recited the wrong blessing, the blessing for fruit that grows on the ground. Had she recited the proper blessing for the date which grows on a tree he would have been completely ameliorated.[15]

Reincarnation was important in Ftayya's thought and piety, and he recorded a number of dreams in which reincarnation is a motif. At the office of the ophthalmologist Ezekiel Ezra ben Moses, Ftayya, who was there as a patient, was asked to interpret the doctor's dream of the previous night. The doctor had dreamt of his father, who had died thirty years ago. In this dream, the only one he ever had about his father, he was asked to accompany his father to the city of Basra. The dream depressed the doctor. Ftayya's interpretation was that the deceased father, because of a violation of a piety (not specified) during his lifetime, had been punished by being incarnated in the body of a man who was sick in "his eyes or bones." The sick man, too poor to pay a doctor's fee, "will come to you today or tomorrow." And Ftayya explained, "Your father came to you [in the dream] to beseech you not to rebuke the man but to help him and not to charge him [a fee]; for he is your [incarnated] father. And the whole thing will occur during a period of three or four days, about as much time as it takes to go from here [Baghdad] to Basra." Ftayya asked the doctor to inform him as soon as it occurred. Upon returning home from his visit at the doctor's office Ftayya received a message that the indigent patient had indeed just come to the doctor's office, that he was impoverished by virtue of his charitableness to others, and that the doctor treated him and gave him money.[16]

Reincarnation was a factor in the dream of a man who, because of piety, had fasted every day but Sabbath. His eating on the Sabbath gave him an upset stomach so he planned to fast also on the Sabbath after receiving rabbinic permission. Before seeking this permission, however, he had a dream in which two men appeared, each bringing a dish, one dish containing fruit from a tree, the other fruit from the ground. Twice the men commanded the dreamer, "Arise and eat," but he refused because he was fasting. "The men became very angry and said to each other, 'take the dish from him because he does not believe in the resurrection of the dead.' " Deeply disturbed by this dream because it implied that he would not be among those resurrected in the future, he sent a message to Ftayya requesting that the dream be interpreted. Ftayya's interpretation was that many souls of people who during their lifetime ate food without reciting a blessing were reincarnated in various foods. A person reciting a blessing before eating ameliorated the soul in the food so that it could enter Gehinnom and be ultimately redeemed. But this dreamer could not ameliorate the lot of those reincarnated souls since he fasted all week and, therefore, could not recite blessings over food. The message of the dream was that he should not fast, that he should eat in order to "resurrect the dead that were reincarnated in that food." The dream figures' statement meant only that the dreamer was not concerned about the *reincarnated souls* achieving resurrection.[17]

Ftayya interpreted a variety of dreams. During a plague in Baghdad, the mother of a learned scholar in the *yeshivah* where Ftayya taught died. Two nights later this scholar, Ezekiel the Persian, dreamed that his father's right eye had been destroyed. Ezekiel came to the *yeshivah* "all atremble" (because as firstborn son he was "his father's right eye" and therefore he, too, might die), asking Ftayya the meaning of his dream. Ftayya's interpretation was that the head phylactery of Ezekiel's father had a flaw in it, and Ftayya told Ezekiel where the flaw was on the parchment. Ftayya knew this because *eye* in the dream is the *gematria* equivalent of one particular word on the first line of a certain section of the parchment of the head phylactery. Over the objection of Ezekiel that the phylactery had been examined the previous month and not found defective, Ftayya insisted that it was defective. Ezekiel rushed home and returned with the phylactery. Ftayya opened the phylactery, took out the parchment that he claimed was defective, and before all the assembled students pointed out the defect. His interpretation was vindicated.[18]

A pregnant woman came to have her dream interpreted. She had dreamed that her husband had gone to the cemetery, disintered his brother's corpse, and brought it home. She insisted that he remove the corpse but he took it up to the roof and buried it. Ftayya's immediate response was to ask the woman how many steps there were from the courtyard of her house up to the roof. She did not know. At Ftayya's suggestion that there were nine steps, she insisted that there were more, probably twelve. Ftayya refused to interpret the dream unless she went home, counted the steps, and returned and told him the correct number. She did, having counted nine stairs. His interpretation, then, of the dream was that she was pregnant with a male child, the reincarnation of her husband's deceased brother, who should be given the brother's name. Ftayya added, "They [sic] inform you that you will complete your nine months of pregnancy, which are the nine steps; you will not abort. He [the child] will live, not die like his uncle, but will ultimately be buried with you in the house and will not be buried in the cemetery." For his reader Ftayya adds, "So it was" and that the woman later thanked him.[19]

Not all clients were genuine. This was the case of an old woman who sought Ftayya's interpretation of a dream. She had dreamed that she was carrying the Torah scroll in the synagogue to the place from which she would read it before the congregation. Another woman came and grabbed it from her. Ftayya's interpretation was that she would be given an infant to be carried to the place designated for the circumcision ceremony. The woman's response to the interpretation was that this had actually transpired two weeks ago and that Ftayya's interpretation did not amount to much. When she added that the dream occurred a month previously, he remarked that she should have come immediately after the dream's occurrence.[20]

For his reader Ftayya added:

> Know, the rule is that a Torah scroll [in a dream] indicates a male child. Therefore, if [in a dream] a man sees that he has acquired a Torah or that they brought him a Torah, the interpretation is that his wife will become pregnant with a male child. If a Torah falls from his hand his wife will abort, if torn the child will die. This interpretation is tried and tested.[21]

To this observation he added some generalizations about dream interpretation. There are, he says,

> other dreams that come in a confused state, disordered; there is no fear or anxiety in them. These dreams come from the forming of the thoughts

of the brain; for the brain is not settled nor at rest from thoughts even during the period of sleep. These dreams are not to be regarded; they do not indicate anything – neither good nor bad. One need not be anxious about them. These are some of the ways of the dreams, "That the wise man may hear, and increase in learning" [Proverbs 1:5].[22]

Ftayya must have kept a dream diary since he recorded a number of dreams that he had in the course of years. In some cases the date of the dream is also given.

His earliest reported dream occurred on a Tuesday night, the twenty-third of *Kislev*, 1899. A *tzaddik* whom he did not know, yet he recognized him as a *tzaddik*, presented a kabbalistic disquisition on prayer and pieties in this dream. Ftayya quoted this at length and added, "All the things that the man said to me he also showed me before my eyes."[23]

He had two dreams during a Sabbath afternoon nap in the month of *Shevat*, 1913. He dreamed that he was strolling in the grain market and noticed two dogs barking at each other. He realized that each dog embodied a reincarnated soul, one the soul of a 50-year-old baker and the other, smaller dog, the soul of a 45-year-old baker: "They sense that they are human beings that dwell in the dogs; they want to speak to each other but cannot. [They can communicate] only by the movements of the organs of the mouth and tongue of the dog. Therefore they bark." Ftayya noticed that they were aware of the fact that he recognized them and so they slunk off in embarrassment. He did not know the sin that caused their condign punishment. After this dream he recalled a kabbalistic tradition that the soul of a man who had intercourse with a gentile woman is reincarnated in a dog.[24]

He fell asleep again on that Sabbath afternoon in 1913 and dreamed of a baker, Ezra ben Asher. Ftayya and Ezra had been childhood friends back in 1865 when they were 6 years old, but they had not seen each other until this very year. In the dream that Sabbath afternoon Ezra and the ten men surrounding him, all properly dressed in shrouds, approached Ftayya. They were on their way to Gehinnom and Ezra asked Ftayya to rescue them from that place, or at least to ease their pain. Ftayya, during all this, was sitting near the *mikvah*, which he describes in great detail. Upon awakening he went to the synagogue for afternoon prayers and inquired of Ezra's brother, who informed him that exactly six months ago Ezra had passed away. Ftayya concluded this account with the statement, "After the Sabbath I made for them [Ezra and the men] a *tikkun.*"[25]

A dream occurred in 1919 on a Friday night, the twenty-second of *Shevat.* Ftayya dreamed that he was walking in the East Side, an area of Baghdad in which poor people lived. There could be seen from a distance an enclosure in the shape of an exedra, in which some forty to fifty soldiers who had been in the center of the city were now relaxing. Ftayya described their uniforms and adds that these soldiers were on watch to see what was happening because there had been a plague in a nearby town. The soldiers did not notice Ftayya since he was not near them; but he had the impression that the soldiers had been attacking the populace. He moved back, not having mentioned that he had previously moved forward, to the East Side, near the gate of a poor man's yard where three Jewish old men were standing. Ftayya approached them, complaining and lamenting that during ancient Temple times there were prophets who admonished the people, warning them to repent or face destruction; and the people did so. During the second Temple era there were "men of the holy spirit, or men who acted under holy inspiration [*bat kol*] or men who had true dreams" who would inform the people about the cause of their troubles. But now we are not admonished; we have no prophets. As Ftayya continued in this vein, three soldiers – he abruptly refers to them as "destroyers," with the connotation of angels – approached. They explained that there was a plague to punish people for eating non-kosher meat and for eating meat and dairy dishes together in gentile and Jewish hotels and in their very own homes.

Although they were called "destroyers," the soldiers did have compassion; but they also had a hit list of transgressors to be punished if they did not repent. Other sinners, unlisted but encountered, may be dealt with as the destroyers see fit. Some of these cases may be sent up to the Heavenly Tribunal for review, since the destroyers do not want to be too destructive. After a rather meandering *apologia pro vita sua,* they tell the dreaming Ftayya:

> Should you be in doubt about these words of ours saying, "it is but a dream and must be disregarded," we will give you a sign and you will

know that it is true. When you and two others will speak to someone who eats non-kosher meat and warn him not to eat it and the man refuses [to obey], tell him, "because you refuse we therefore decree that on such and such a day and at such and such an hour you will die." [When that happens,] you will know that this was a true dream.[26]

These destroyers left and another group of 120 destroyers arrived, complaining about their unnecessary task, since the first group of destroyers had finished the work. The dream ended with these destroyers about to leave. Ftayya added the postscript that on Wednesday, the 4th of Adar, the plague ceased in the Jewish community but was still raging in the gentile community.

Another dream of his occurred in 1919. First he recounted the events that preceded the dream. The first Sabbath of the month of *Av* of that year he spent away from home in the city of Ba'quba. His host induced him to pay a condolence call to a bereaved old couple whose adult son, an only child, had been killed by gentile brigands. The couple implored him to account for their loss and asked him whether their son had been reincarnated. He tried to console them, saying that on his return home he would search the kabbalistic works and give them an answer. On Monday, the eighth of *Av*, he returned home. On the morning of the ninth he was in the synagogue and during the recitation of the laments he dozed and dreamed about the murdered young man. In this dream he saw the entire incident, which he describes in great detail; and he also saw what happened to the soul of that young man in its ascent to the Heavenly Tribunal, before whom it successfully petitioned that it be avenged. Ftayya "saw the whole thing from the beginning to its end," and he wrote a letter to the bereaved parents explaining all this.[27]

In 1925 (the specific night is not given) Ftayya dreamed of an old man who had initially come to him seeking help in 1923 because of the sin of intercourse with a daughter-in-law. In the dream Ftayya saw the man standing before the Heavenly Tribunal. Three angels who were "healers" operated on the sinner's membrum and "cured him entirely" so that he achieved atonement.[28]

Some of Ftayya's dreams are of historical interest, since they bear witness to ordinarily unexpressed, somewhat heretical, concerns.

Ftayya was a very learned talmudist and kabbalist. He was a

teacher at a *yeshivah*, a Talmud academy in Baghdad. He was a traditional Jew. Yet some of his dreams reveal a deep sympathy with Sabbatianism. This is expressed in the dreams he had of Nathan of Gaza.

In his comments to Isaiah 30:33, Ftayya interprets *hearth* as meaning Gehinnom, and after a long digression about the deceased righteous ones also experiencing the punishments in that place, he says Nathan of Gaza also had to enter it. Ftayya elaborates by telling of a dream he had on a Sunday night, the eve of the twenty-fifth of *Kislev* (Hanukkah), 1911. He had been telling his family about the miracle of Hanukkah as discussed in the book *Hemdat Yamim* when he dozed and had a dream. A chubby, attractive man, beardless but for a few scraggly hairs, and about 45 years old, appeared. He stood in back of Ftayya, off to the left (for Kabbalah, the left connotes evil). The man in the dream whispered in Ftayya's ear, "I am the author of *Hemdat Yamim*; hearken unto me, conduct yourself as I conduct myself [to which Ftayya added: that I should believe in the accursed Shabbetai Tzvi that he is the messiah, God forbid]; and I will teach you all the four sections of *Hemdat Yamim* in a moment." At Ftayya's doubts about the feasibility of this, Nathan of Gaza continued:

> Know that when I composed *Hemdat Yamim* I was attached to Shabbetai Zevi and I conducted myself guardedly as he conducted himself. It was my desire to attract the hearts of Israel to him but I decided that they would not listen to me. Therefore, I devised a great strategy and composed *Hemdat Yamim* . . . with the hope that all Israel will follow Shabbetai Zevi.[29]

Ftayya awoke knowing, of course, that the man in the dream was Nathan of Gaza because Ftayya "knew" that Nathan had composed that book.

Two nights later he dreamed again. In his dream it was a cold Sabbath afternoon; he was dressed in a wool cloak seated on a wool carpet in a room and studying *The Tree of Life*. Strewn around were some twenty volumes that he consulted as he studied. Suddenly he saw a very large raven, twice as large as others. It was flying but appeared to be confused, as if injured by those pursuing it. The raven was so afraid that it came to Ftayya and hid under his woolen cloak. Then three men appeared with staffs that had been used to attack the raven. They were very angry at not finding the raven, which remained hidden under Ftayya's cloak. Suddenly Ftayya was aware of the leader of these men proclaiming, "The Gazites saying, 'Nathan is come hither,' " and pointing out to the men the raven hidden under Ftayya's cloak. Having heard the leader's statement and its substitution of *Nathan* for the biblical verse's *Samson* (Judges 16:2), Ftayya understood that the raven was Nathan of Gaza. The raven flew off, pursued by the men, and Ftayya woke up.

But he fell asleep and again dreamed of Nathan of Gaza. In the dream it was a weekday and he was in the synagogue, sitting in his usual place, when Nathan of Gaza appeared, imploring Ftayya to ameliorate his condition, for he was in a perilous state, "as you have seen, with your eyes, that raven." Ftayya adds that in the dream he had nodded to Nathan that he would do his best to help him.[30] Four days later Ftayya gathered together twelve *yeshivah* students and conducted a long prayer service, the text of which he includes, to ameliorate Nathan's condition.[31]

On the eve of the second of the month of *Shevat*, less than two months after the earlier dreams about Nathan, Ftayya dreamed that an emissary of Nathan of Gaza appeared, reciting, "It is burned with fire, it is cut down" (Psalm 80:17), which Ftayya interpreted as meaning that Nathan had entered Gehinnom. The emissary, not understanding that this was the beginning of the amelioration of Nathan's soul, was sad but he showed Ftayya Nathan's joyous approach to the netherworld and the problems on the way.[32]

Missing from Ftayya's hermeneutics are references to the Talmud's understanding of dreams. Ftayya, a most learned talmudist, interpreted dreams kabbalistically, as if he had never studied tractate *Berakhot*, the locus classicus of Jewish dream interpretation. The Talmud's statement that "dreams follow the mouth"[33] of the interpreter is never referred to by Ftayya. And despite the fact that he was a "professional" dream interpreter, he did not refer to the biblical Joseph's dream interpretations in the eight pages devoted to Genesis, chapters 40 and 41 in *Minhat Yehudah*.

That he did not refer to the Talmud's "dreams follow the mouth" does not mean that he was unaware of this observation. He presupposed it. For it is this very idea that accounts for his certainty that his interpretations were always valid; the interpretations he gave his clients were valid for they followed his mouth.

It is nevertheless worth noting that he did not reflect, as did Almoli, for example, on the problematics of the Talmud's statement. The issue of subjectivity and relativism versus "truth" was not confronted by Ftayya.

Since Ftayya's *Minhat Yehudah* is a commentary on selected biblical verses (and a citation or two from Talmud and *Zohar*), it is surprising that he did not comment on Numbers 6:24–27, the Priestly Blessing that, when chanted by the priests in the synagogue, is the time for the recitation of the prayer about dreams.

Nor did he ever suggest to any of his clients that there was a traditional prayer service for the amelioration of dreams. One would have expected him to do so since Ftayya, a traditional Jew of great learning, was also, in a sense, a therapist. People who were haunted by evil spirits came to him for help. Ftayya not only exorcised these spirits, but he also helped these haunted people (and even the spirits) by suggesting pious regimens for them to follow that would relieve them of their troubles.[34]

Indeed, Ftayya was so much the therapist that he has been described as

> sitting every day at the entrance of his house and receiving the lads [who studied under him], and their mothers, to bless them. Many [others] visited him before they went to a doctor; they would tell him their story, he would bless them and advise them to go also to the doctor. Every one who visited him believed in his blessing and [thereby] was cured.[35]

It is surprising, therefore, that he did not suggest that his clients also attend the synagogue for a service of dream amelioration.

These clients were representative of various classes in the community. Even the small number of examples would indicate this. He interpreted, as cited above, the dreams of a sage, a working woman, various old men and old women, an ophthalmologist, and students.

Ftayya, dream interpreter and "therapist," was a person of consequence in Baghdad in the latter part of the nineteenth and first third of
the twentieth centuries. He was a learned sage of importance in
Baghdad's Jewish traditional academic institutions. There were a
number of *yeshivot* in Baghdad, each one housed in a synagogue. In the
synagogue Bet Midrash Zilkah there were nine such academies, one of
which was the "*Yeshivah* of Rabbi Judah Ftayya." In this synagogue
there were also a number of "night *yeshivot*" that were attended by
learned adult laymen. One of these nighttime academies had been
established by Ftayya for the study of Hayim Vital's *Tree of Life*. Ftayya
founded another night *yeshivah* that met in the Elijah Reuben synagogue and was attended by a large number of businessmen.

Ftayya was well occupied in the life of the community: "He was
well known. Everyone called him 'Judah, the Sage,' without any other
designation or surname. He did this [blessing people, advising them to
see a physician] for the sake of heaven, *despite all the bother and fuss in the
morning* immediately after the morning prayers [emphasis added]."[36]

His importance is also indicated by a number of photographs.
One, reproduced a number of times, was taken in Baghdad in 1910 and
is captioned "The Sages of Baghdad." Ftayya, one of twelve, is
standing in the second row, and like the others, is dressed in the
traditional robes of Baghdad rabbis and sages.[37]

In a 1922 photograph, Ftayya is the only rabbi seated among nine
laymen, one of whom is the emissary from Keren Hayesod.[38] He also
appears in a 1924 photograph of Rabbi Ezra Dangoor, chief rabbi of
Baghdad, and the Jewish court, at the dedication of a wing of a
hospital.[39]

In a montage, not dated, entitled "The Sages of Iraq of the Last
Generation," Ftayya is one of the fourteen sages pictured.[40]

Judah Ftayya, talmudist and kabbalist, therapist and dream interpreter, was so affected by dreams that a major work of his was
composed as a result of a dream. In the introduction to his *Bet Lehem
Yehudah*, a commentary to Vital's *Tree of Life*, he notes that during the
period of mourning for Rabbi Simon Agasi, who died three days before
the outbreak of the First World War, he was approached by an elder.

The elder told Ftayya that he had a disturbing dream the previous night but categorically refused to tell Ftayya what he had seen in the dream:

> Only this did he say: that they [*sic*] said to him in the dream that they agreed in the Upper World about you [Ftayya] being the replacement of our colleague R. Simon and that with all [your] might [you] must strive for the good of the city; the thought that entered your mind last night, while lying down, to study the books of our colleague R. Simon, you must strive actually to achieve it.

The elder then left Ftayya but returned two hours later, urging Ftayya to go to Agasi's home and take the books needed for study. To this Ftayya added that "I now know the intent of the dream: they hint at the study of the *Tree of Life*." Subsequently, he began the study of that great work, most intensely, and to practice devotional and charitable works, which finally led to his deciding to write a commentary to the *Tree of Life*.[41]

5

AN AMERICAN-YIDDISH
INTERPRETATION OF DREAMS

In 1907, in New York, there was published a thirty-two-page book with the Hebrew title *Pitron Halomot*, subtitled, in Yiddish, "Or: Dream Book." Underneath this was the following statement in Yiddish: "A book that teaches [one] how to interpret the dreams that occur to different people and also how to distinguish which dreams have a meaning from those which do not." Beneath this, in Yiddish, was the statement, "Written in Hebrew by the scholar and philosopher R. Isaac [*sic*! not Solomon] Almoli, translated into Yiddish by A. B."[1]

This "translator,"[2] whose name is not given, did know Solomon Almoli's sixteenth-century *Interpretation of Dreams*, which had been republished as recently as 1902 in Warsaw. A. B., however, did not translate it, nor did he so much as rework it. This is readily apparent when one compares the two books. A. B. used Almoli's book but he composed his own work. Despite its brevity of thirty-two pages, while Almoli's is one hundred pages long, A. B.'s book is of historical interest in its own right.

A. B. had thought about the psychology of dreams. In the first section, "What is a Dream?" he explains that dreams occur when "our limbs are tired, the eyes close themselves, and we fall into the arm[s] of sleep. This time is most necessary in our unknown *dazein* [existence] in order to gather strength for the life that lies ahead." In the course of diurnal life "the soul is one with the body in its task of regulating" the body. During sleep, however,

> this obligation falls away from the soul [*seele*] . . . the soul or the *neshamah* [another Yiddish word, from Hebrew, for *soul*] remains, there-fore, inactive and becomes separated [from the body] unto her own "I" of self-existence. This *seele* or *neshamah* which however is a "portion of the divine from above" being free of bodily tasks . . . has times when she can see and feel things that occur or will occur which concern only this body or other people.[3]

A. B. develops this idea by distinguishing two personality types. One type has two variations. There is the person who has very little to do with the world and is not concerned about it; "this soul has nothing to do with alien things other than the body which she manages."[4] Examples are the two imprisoned servants of the biblical Pharaoh, dreaming of things relating only to them. The other variation is the mediocre person with a mediocre soul. A. B.'s example is Joseph and his brothers; "they [*sic*] had dreamed about things that affected their family life, and nothing more,"[5] a strange statement by A. B., a learned man who knew that Joseph's brothers did not dream and that Joseph's dreams were of significance in the course of Israelite history.

There is, however, another kind of personality type: the person whose dreams have an impact on the world. That dreamer is a king. Pharaoh's dreams in contrast to those of his servants; Nebuchadnez-zar's dream, "which could never have been dreamed in a beggar's dream" because Nebuchadnezzar "was a powerful king who subdued a whole world, therefore his soul saw things that will be played out hundreds or thousands of years later."[6]

At this point in his *Interpretation of Dreams*, A. B. forgoes discussing this type of dreamer, the great historic figure who dreams great dreams of historical significance. His book was written primarily for the ordinary, self-centered, mediocre person. Only in his last chapter will he discuss the great dreamer again.

This section concludes with this passage:

We return again to the substance of the dream. A dream is mostly the picture of the future for one's self or for others, which our soul conceives . . . the picture of the hidden [*geheimnes*] future that human eyes cannot see and human reason cannot view, only our soul alone. This divine portion is able to conceive everything and to tear down the curtain from that which will occur in the future.[7]

The next chapter, "The Difference in Dreams," makes a number of interesting points. Not all dreams are to be interpreted; they do not necessarily indicate what will happen in the future or what will happen to someone else. "The body when it is asleep makes a great impression upon our brain," which can make for dreams that have no meaning. And the stomach as a result of sickness or when full of strong drink or heavy food can cause one to have "frightful dreams or wild, confused thoughts because the blood must work too hard for the stomach, and in the coursing of the blood through the body it impedes the pure work of the brain which is the instrument of the soul [*neshamah*]."[8]

The dreams that one has because of these factors are of no concern. Something else also has a role in dreaming. The brain can be affected by one's "reading wild stories about bandits, robbers, murderers; this happens particularly when we [*sic*] read such [stories] before sleeping."[9] This observation by A. B. is something that Almoli in the sixteenth century, an era without daily newspapers and magazines, could not have made. Sorrow and bad luck, according to A. B., can also have an effect upon the brain.

These things should be kept in mind; A. B. admonishes

the dreamer to look around first, before he goes to investigate the meaning of the dream, as to whether this [dream] has not come in a time when the soul [*neshamah*] is not free to handle [it] alone. A dream that occurs and is caused by the body has no meaning; every sensible person need not be alarmed by it.

Addressing his reader, A. B. says:

Now we will approach the right dream about which we can search for meaning. Such dreams are so important that their meaning plays, sometimes, the greatest role in our very own life or in the life of others. And it has happened, already many times, that people have as a result been enabled to avoid misfortune or to save others from misfortune.[10]

The next section, "The Dream and the Interpreter," consisting of two and a half pages, begins with a quotation from the Talmud, the source of which he notes: "A man cannot see in a dream neither a golden tree nor how an elephant crawls in through the eye of a needle." He considers this rabbinic statement "a great truth" because, while many fantastic things can be seen while dreaming, "things that have never been in the world" cannot be seen in a dream.[11]

Furthermore, although dreams portray the future, this is shown by things in the present. A. B. also makes the point that ordinary things that one confronts in daily life are of no significance when seen in dreams. When, for instance, a cobbler dreams of a pair of shoes, it does not mean anything, nor when the tailor dreams of trousers, nor when the blacksmith dreams of horseshoes. "But it is noteworthy when an ordinary, tranquil man sees himself in a dream wrestling with a bear, or a woman dreams that she has choked a lion." As an example of a dream that is of unusual things he tells of a dream that an Italian woman had "at the close of the seventeenth century."[12] Dreaming that her lover was being killed by his brother, and being urged by a voice to go and warn her lover, she does so and thereby saves him.

Of course, A. B. concluded, where meanings are so "clear," as the Italian woman's dream, there is no need for an interpreter.

Generally, however, dreams do need an interpreter, "and much depends on such a person." A. B. proceeds to explain the importance of interpretation: "The Gemara says in one place that 'A wise man is even superior to a prophet' and in another place, 'All dreams follow the mouth.' Much depends on the interpreter, if he is a person of sense."[13]

And A. B. stresses that

> the interpretation of a dream cannot be changed. A dream is not ambiguous; but a dream may sometimes have bad consequences when it is not given the right interpretation . . . An incorrect interpretation may cause the dreamer so much concern that it can make him sick from sorrow or make for suicide in order that he [the dreamer] avoid beggaring.[14]

This chapter then concludes with, "This is what is meant by 'All dreams follow the mouth' or better said 'Life and death are in the power of the tongue.' A person of sense or a right kind of interpreter would not commit such stupidity, [i.e.,] to scare a person."[15]

After a brief passage distinguishing dreams that come true in the near future from those that take time to materialize, A. B. presents "Sections," each of which contains interpretations of the meaning of a class of objects seen in dreams. The chapter headings of these sections were taken from Almoli's *Interpretation of Dreams*, but the contents, the symbols interpreted, are by and large different from Almoli's. Almoli's "[If in a dream] one erects a door at the entrance of his home he will soon marry"[16] is for A. B. "If [in a dream] one places a door or a window in his home, he will either marry very soon, or if already married, his wife will become pregnant."[17]

The rubric of this first section, "Concerning Things Which are Inanimate," is Almoli's. Almoli referred to dreams of travel to various lands in the Near East, including the Land of Israel. A. B., however, interprets traveling in various directions and a note not found in Almoli: "Seeing myself [in a dream] in a land where Jews are hated is a sign that one will not be able to free oneself from the misery which is coming."[18]

In this section of three and a half pages, A. B. includes objects that Almoli interpreted, for example, a coin, jewels, and so forth. But A. B., for instance, interpreted jewels in a dream differently from Almoli. Pearls in a dream means, according to A. B., that one's wife or sister is "carrying on immorally with one about whom [the dreamer] has his suspicions," and jewels indicate that "the woman one loves will find another [lover]."[19] Almoli's interpretations of jewels do not refer to woman, love, or sex.

For A. B., "A woman or a girl who dreams too frequently about precious jewelry must expect that her husband will lose his money in card games."[20] Women, for the most part wives, are referred to frequently in this section in connection with the objects seen in men's dreams. Objects indicate a wife's innocence, a wife's falseness, a woman's need for love. Some objects mean strife in the family; crosses and images of the divine indicate that best friends are false friends.[21] Thse things are not referred to in Almoli's book.

The section "Concerning Various Flora" is also borrowed from Almoli's *Interpretation of Dreams*, but the content is different. In this three-and-a-half-page section there is a subheading: "Concerning Wood Ships and Iron Ships." Almoli had included wood ships because wood is produced by flora. A. B. followed this but also included iron ships, something that Almoli in the sixteenth century did not know, since until the eighteenth century there were no iron ships.

In A. B.'s *Interpretation of Dreams*, "Eating fruit in a garden means that he [the dreamer] will have a bad reputation"; a somewhat similar dream indicates that one's wife is "false" and is involved with another man. "A woman dreaming of eating fruit [in a garden] and someone grabs it from her means that her husband is licentious and associates with other women; her dreaming that she is eating fruit and someone asks for a portion means that a woman about whom she has her suspicions will steal her husband away." But if she does not give the requested portion, "there is no doubt" that the woman "had already carried on immorally with the dreamer's husband."[22] "When a woman dreams of oranges [it means that] her husband's love for her is very great; of lemons she should take care [and see to it] that he spends less time meeting with women." A man dreaming of lemons indicates that his wife should get together "less frequently with men."[23] In this section, too, some adult dreams refer to children and their problems. None of these things is found in Almoli's book.

A. B.'s section on ships has very little that is borrowed. His concluding sentence of this brief account is not found in Almoli but is characteristic of A. B.: "Seeing oneself [in a dream] as a castaway from a ship to an island means that one will be separated from one's family."[24]

In the third section of four and a half pages, "Concerning Different Animals," the rubric and some of the material are Almoli's. An ox or a sheep "means that what one does will turn out to be successful."[25] For Almoli such a dream meant "[things will be] good for him."[26] For A. B., "Eating horse meat [not kosher] in a dream meant that one will have a good year."[27] A. B. took this from Almoli but he omitted something important for Almoli: "One who sees [himself] eating the flesh of a horse, *Ha-Shem* [God] will ordain his food for him;

and his funds will be guarded."[28] A. B. intentionally omitted Almoli's piously stated reference to God.

In this section dealing with animals in dreams, among his interpretations are the following: "Ripped by a tiger means that one's beloved is false and he will be ruined by her . . . Licked by a dog [means] that a relative, male or female, loves the dreamer and is too embarrassed to confess it."[29]

Here, as in the flora section, Woman as dreamer or as object in dreams is noted frequently. A. B. is so aware of Woman's existence as being different from Man's existence that he interprets the same dream differently when dreamed by them. "Grabbed by a cat [means] that one's wife will bring about misfortune." And "when a woman dreams that she was grabbed by a cat she should conclude that her sister or best friend will take her lover away from her."[30]

A. B. understood Woman's wishes and weaknesses, at least as he assumed them to be:

> When a woman dreams that she has fought with a lion and conquered [it means] that men will lie at her feet and will bow down to her beauty or to her understanding. When the woman dreams that a lion has conquered her then she will fall victim to lust . . . When a woman dreams that she is playing with cats and dogs she must guard herself from the man she loves because he will make her unlucky.

But when a man dreams of "playing with dogs [it means] that he will be loved by women." For either sex, however, "Seeing animals coupling means that one will suffer much because of lust."[31]

Although Almoli's *Interpretation of Dreams* has material on "Lying With Women," he was not particularly given to interpreting dreams as having sexual significance, nor did he interpret the dreams by women.

In A. B.'s book family tensions are, in some instances, expressed in dreams. The following two characterize the concerns of an early-twentieth-century immigrant Jewish community in New York:

> Seeing a bird [in a dream] rising from the ground, rising higher and higher and becoming larger each time means that the dreamer's child

will overwhelm the world with wonderful things. Dreaming that a pigeon turned into an eagle and flew up to the sun [means] that the dreamer's only child will become a great thinker and will astound the world with his wisdom.[32]

The next section, not found in Almoli, is "Concerning Angels and Demons." His brief introduction is important. He refers to

> an earlier observation of ours that those things that do not exist in nature do not occur in dreams; or better stated, those things not seen while awake cannot be seen while dreaming. Nevertheless people have actually dreamed of having seen demons or angels. It is not here a question as to whether or not demons or angels exist. The important thing is: how does one see them in a dream since no one has seen them while awake![33]

A. B. is skeptical of supernatural beings. He does not refer to God or to prophetic dreams, and has hardly any examples or quotations from religious texts. But he is very much aware of folk fears and experiences and feels obliged to deal with dreams about angels and demons. He is pragmatic. These supernatural beings

> are actually not seen in a dream because one does not see them while awake. What one does see [in a dream] is either what one has represented to oneself in fantasy while awake or what one has seen in a picture. One must be discriminating about such a dream as to whether it is not the result of excitement during the day. If it is only this then it has no meaning. When, however, he [the angel or demon] appears without having been caused by them the following interpretations are possible.[34]

Of his four interpretations of angels and demons doing different things, the following two for each being are representative:

> Seeing demons dance means one should be careful to see to it that the children do not bathe in deep water . . . Demons making jokes and laughing means that one will quarrel with his wife or with his business partner; and, in either case, nothing good will result . . . Angels taking

things away signifies that one's best friend is persuading the dreamer's wife to run away with him. Angels bringing beautiful things means that one will fall victim to women's beauty.[35]

The next section, not found in Almoli, interprets "Milk, Cheese, Butter, Honey, and Breasts." Ten interpretations are presented. Two deal with women's breasts. One meaning is that the dreamer "will steal, will be captured, and will be dishonored." Another meaning is that the dreamer "will be able to withstand the temptation." Eating butter means one "will derive pleasure from children." Eating cheese means "one will suffer from children."[36]

A. B.'s section on "The Dead" is different in content from Almoli's. His brief introduction betrays his skepticism. It begins with a categorical statement: "Ninety-nine percent of the dreams about the dead are the result of thinking about them [as they were] during their lifetime." And he suggests that the dreamer be very "discriminating" in determining whether such a dream "has in it something real and [only then] seek a clarification." He indicates that with this stricture in mind he gives his interpretations. Of seven, two are the following: "The dead crying [means] there will be joy in the home. Deceased parents appearing always has a good meaning."[37]

Parallel to Almoli's section on clothes, A. B.'s fourth section is "Concerning People and What Belongs To Them." Among his interpretations are the following: "Seeing a man's hidden organs [signifies] there will be luck in the household; a woman's [signifies] there will be great conflicts . . . Feeling one's teeth growing [means] a child will become ill." One's nose cut off means the dreamer "will be afflicted by his enemies."[38] A woman who dreams that her "breasts are cut off will have no more children." Dreaming that one is barefoot means that "one will have great lust." And "a man dreaming that he is involved with a woman who is a stranger signifies that he will stop loving his wife. . . . A woman who sees in a dream that she has married a man who is a stranger signifies that her husband will mistrust her."[39] A. B.'s "seeing oneself naked [in a dream signifies] that one's wife will steal from him" is very different from the Talmud's interpretation that it means piety/impiety, depending on the locale of the dream.[40]

The fifth section, "Concerning Heavenly Bodies and Natural

Phenomena," is parallel to Almoli's but briefer. Both interpret sun, moon, stars, and so forth, in dreams. Almoli, however, included such heavenly things as Torah and other parts of Scripture, which A. B., of course, ignores.

There are two final sections in A. B.'s *Interpretation of Dreams*: "Concerning Frightful Dreams and Their Meanings" and "Concerning Dreams of Great Meaning."

The first of these, consisting of three pages, is strikingly different from the earlier parts of this book. Nearly two full pages are devoted to an account of an incident that took place, according to him, in Paris during 1798. Without giving his source, A. B. tells of Jean Rivall, "a famous dream interpreter and his interpretation of the dream dreamt by the Count de Valentine," a valid interpretation in that the nobleman, as a result of the interpretation, realized his wife's unfaithfulness when he found her in a hotel with his best friend, Henri Artun, and killed her.

This story is told in great detail, and it concludes with an excerpt from Rivall's "writings about dreams": "Undoubtedly had I interpreted differently for him the young wife would, perhaps, not have lost her life." And Rivall is quoted as having made the same observation about another of his dream interpretations that turned out to be correct.[41]

This rather lengthy account serves A. B. in making his point: "All this demonstrates the great truth of the Gemara's assertion that 'All dreams follow the mouth'; and one must be very careful in interpreting particularly a frightful dream, because this can lead to a very serious and dangerous consequence."[42]

A. B.'s *Interpretation of Dreams* has at least two foci: Everyman and the Oneirocritic. "The dreams and their interpretations which we had previously enumerated are still not all that people are capable of dreaming; however it suffices for reasonable people."[43]

And the second focus:

> This book [however] is not just for laymen [*privat menschen*] but for folk who are interested in becoming dream interpreters. We say to them that they should thoroughly study our earlier chapters and should patiently read through our last chapter. Every word is useful and interesting. And one should heed the following rules:

(1) Has the dream occurred after an excitement, sickness, or heavy food–then it has no meaning.

(2) Is the dream about an object with which one works–then it has no meaning.

(3) When the dream is clear, not overblown, then the meaning lies in the plain content.

(4) When the dream occurs with surprise and leaves behind a restless temper it is best not to interpret while the spirit [*geist*] of the dreamer is not calm.

(5) The interpreter should, at any rate, seek to give a good interpretation instead of an evil one; since as long as the evil one cannot be avoided it is not necessary to tell it. As long as one can avoid [telling it] it is better to present the good side.

(6) People who often dream bad dreams should be warned not to drink strong liquor, not to eat heavy food, and that it is better to go to sleep hungry rather than sated. Such [people] should also not read any exciting romances and should not attend exciting shows in the theatre.[44]

There is, however, another focus to A. B.'s *Interpretation of Dreams*. He begins his final chapter, "Concerning Dreams of Great Significance," by noting that early on in the book he pointed out that ordinary people have ordinary dreams of no great significance. "But," he now asserts, "progressive people have other opportunities in life and, therefore, dreams can show them great things."[45]

To substantiate this he tells of an occurrence in Mantua, Italy, "some three hundred years ago," recorded in a Hebrew book, *D'shaynim V'Raananim*.[46] A most learned young man, Hayyim Esperero, dreamed that a gentile high-ranking army man who had made life difficult for Jews was drowning in the Tiber river in Rome. In the dream, Hayyim Esperero rescued the man. Hayyim subsequently informed the rabbi of Mantua of his dream and went to Rome, where he stood watch at the Tiber every day. On the thirty-third day, he saved a cardinal who was a very important member of the curia from drowning. This was a time when 216 Jews in Rome had been imprisoned because they were accused of killing a Christian child and using his blood. Because he rescued the cardinal, Hayyim Esperero managed to get the Jews freed and declared innocent of all charges. He was also handsomely rewarded by the cardinal, became wealthy, and was in a position of great help to the Jews.

A. B. recounts this story, much of it a long quotation from the book, and adds his own assessment: "Had Hayyim Esperero not interested himself in that important dream [of his] and not told it to the rabbi and had not gone to Rome, he would not have, first of all, saved his poor brethren; and, secondly, he would not have personally become important."[47]

Following his summing up of the story, A. B. concludes his book with an admonishment: "People with dreams which appear to have great significance must not at any price neglect the opportunity [they have] and [should] attain the goal that such dreams have pointed out."[48]

A. B. had indicated that there are different kinds of dreams as there are different types of people. A king's dreams are about his kingdom. A commoner's dreams are petty, self-centered. A. B.'s *Interpretation of Dreams* serves primarily to interpret the dreams of the common people, the Yiddish-speaking East European immigrant community in America.

He was, however, also interested in significant dreams, dreams that would signify things of import for a community or a commonwealth. And although in the modern world (of his time) there were no great kings known to have had great dreams that he might have cited as examples, there was the dream of Hayyim Esperero. In the quotation about this young man, he is described not only as "learned," which we had noted, but also as "a wise and cultured [*gebildeter*] person and he knew Latin, Italian, and Spanish along with Hebrew and the Talmud and its ancillary material."[49]

While there are no great kings there is, however, the superior person, learned and cultured, who may have a dream with meaning for the life of an historic community. A. B. urges this uncommon person to take the dream seriously, that is, to act upon it.

The idea, the dream of the superior person, is important in this book. It deals with an issue A. B. must have felt he could not avoid: the prophetic dream. As Almoli, in his sixteenth-century *Interpretation of Dreams*, distinguished between the prophetic dream and the ordinary dream, A. B., a secular Jew and an elitist writing for a community literate but not traditionally learned or pious, distinguished between their dreams and the dreams of the superior person. Almoli faced the question as to the source of the dream. And despite the difference between the ordinary and the prophetic dream, ultimately they were both rooted in the divine. For A. B. the dream of the superior person is what the prophetic dream is for the traditional Jew.

A. B. does not so much as mention God. As for angels and demons, they are but figments of the imagination, and the term *ba'al halom* that A. B. uses on occasion is simply one of the standard Yiddish terms for *dreamer.*

The source of the dream is the soul, the *neshamah,* what it "grasps when it does not have to deal with the work of the body."[50] Although the soul is the "divine portion," what it means is never explained.

A. B. was a secular humanist. As God is not referred to, the synagogue is also not mentioned. The synagogue offered dream therapy: the Priestly Blessing with its prayer concerning dreams and the Amelioration of Dreams service. A. B. is silent about these.

Biblical verses play no role in A. B.'s dream interpretation. The one biblical verse he quotes, "Death and life are in the power of the tongue" (Proverbs 18:21), is misquoted because he reverses the order of the first two nouns. And since biblical verses do not serve him, paronomasia is not a method in his oneirocriticism. Since A. B. was not a traditional Jewish thinker, his rejection of the biblical-rabbinic tradition made for his rejection of the Word. Being a "modern" he is a nominalist; words are no more than arbitrary labels, mere utterances having no reality and, therefore, of no hermeneutic significance. What is seen by the dreamer is an object, not a word = thing.

A. B. was a twentieth-century man in a number of ways. Along with his obvious rejection of traditional faith and pieties, his awareness of woman's particular concerns, needs, and yearnings places him among the moderns. In many cases, as was noted, he gives a different interpretation if a dream occured to a woman rather than to a man. Furthermore, he was aware of family strife, tensions between husband and wife and between parents and children, parental concern for a son's career, and the concerns and fears of a recently arrived community of immigrants his is a twentieth-century sensibility.

Most striking is the importance of the erotic in his oneirocriticism. In traditional texts, erotic dreams are not frequently noted. For A. B., however, the erotic, both the dream and/or its interpretation, is an important theme in his *Interpretation of Dreams*.

In her study, *"In Visa Noctus*: Dreams in European Hagiographa And Histories, 450–900,"[51] Lisa M. Bitel states:

> The Germanic peoples of early medieval Europe did not dream as we do. They defined their dreams differently . . . they also used dreams for different purposes and interpreted them in ways that seem odd and sometimes even silly to us. We victims of Freud, for instance, assume that dreams of flying signify the longing for sexual experiences; to medieval dreamers, a dream of flying meant merely a forthcoming change of address for the dreamer.

While A. B. was not one of the "victims of Freud," his twentieth-century world was not the sixteenth-century world of Solomon Al-moli and certainly not the world of the talmudic sages, worlds in which the erotic was not a dominant motif. A. B.'s early-twentieth-century New York Jewish community and Judah Ftayya's late-nineteenth- and twentieth-century Baghdad Jewish community did have, despite vast differences, something in common: erotic dreams and dreams interpreted by these two oneirocritics, unknown as they were to each other, erotically.

May one hazard the suggestion that these two Jewish communities shared this in common with a late-nineteenth- and early twentieth-century European city called Vienna and its oneirocritic?

6

DREAM THERAPY IN JEWISH TRADITION

Dream therapy in Jewish tradition consists of two different procedures: the Priestly Blessing and the Amelioration of Dreams. Both, despite differences, deal with dreams not interpretively but therapeutically.

In traditional synagogues, during holiday services, the priests in the congregation bless the worshipers with the Priestly Blessing, chanted in Hebrew: "The Lord bless thee and keep thee; the Lord make His face to shine upon thee and be gracious unto thee; the Lord lift up His countenance upon thee and give thee peace."[1] The words of this blessing are divinely ordained, and blessing the congregation is a divinely ordained priestly function, according to the tradition.

During the course of the Priestly Blessing, the worshipers twice recite a prayer concerning dreams: "Master of the universe, I am Thine and my dreams are Thine; I have dreamed a dream and I do not know what it is," and continues that if the dreams are "good" dreams may they be "strengthened and be made firm, fulfilled like the dreams of Joseph." If they need "healing," the worshiper asks God to "heal them" as He healed Hezekiah from "his sickness" (Isaiah 38:1–5), Miriam's leprosy (Numbers 12:10–15), Naaman's leprosy (2 Kings 5), and as He "healed" the waters of Marah through Moses (Exodus 23:22–25), the waters of Jericho through Elisha (2 Kings 2:19–22), and "overturned" the curse of Balaam into a blessing (Numbers 22–24) "so may You overturn all my dreams unto the good for me and for all Israel."[2]

The crucial terms are *healing* and *overturning,* but healing is the more important since it is used in reference to three instances of human illness and two instances of bitter waters as compared with only one instance of overturning a curse.

The worshiper asks not for a different dream but for the healing of the dream. That in the prayer only one dreamer, Joseph, is referred to is instructive, for in Scripture there are other references to dreamers. This prayer, the subject of which is dreams, intentionally avoids more than a single example of a dreamer and emphasizes sick people and waters that need therapy. Of the seven people mentioned only one is a dreamer. This is so, I suggest, because in dreaming "the temporal order disintegrates" and "the dreamer is alone in his dream world."[3] Since the dreamer is alone in a situation of temporal disorder, a modality unacceptable for Jewish existence, which is historic-covenantal, there is in this prayer concerning dreams only one reference, therefore, to a dreamer, and five references to healing and one to overturning.

Dreaming is primarily a visual rather than an aural experience. Indeed, the Hebrew word for dream, *halom,* is a visual term.[4] For the dreamer whose impressions are visual the temporal order disintegrates, and "acoustic impressions which require the sequence of time to form a whole cannot as fragmentary presences be used by the dreamer to make up an encompassing meaningful unity."[5] The sequence of time is imperative for aural impressions but not for visual impressions. Furthermore, "sound has process character," is temporally ordered, "and gives only dynamic and never static character . . . discloses . . . not an object but a dynamical event at the focus of sound."[6]

The Priestly Blessing is aural, embodies temporal sequence and, as we shall soon note, rejects the visual. At the appropriate time in the congregation's prayer service the precentor exclaims, "Priests," and they assemble on the platform in front of the congregation, reciting a benediction that concludes with "and commanded us to bless Thy people Israel with love." Here, and in what follows, there is an ordered time-sequence:

First: The precentor exclaims, and the priests chant, the first two
           words of the blessing.
Second: The congregants recite the prayer concerning dreams during
           which time the priests chant a melody and conclude with
           the third word of the blessing.
Third: The precentor exclaims, and the priests chant, the next five
           Hebrew words.
Fourth: The prayer concerning dreams is again recited, the priests
           chanting and concluding the second section of the blessing.
Fifth: The precentor exclaims, and the priests chant, the con-
           cluding words of the blessing.
Sixth: The worshipers and priests each recite a prayer in which
           blessings are asked for the people Israel and the Land of
           Israel.

In this dynamic event, which rejects the visual, things could be seen if
one looks: the priests standing in stockinged feet on the platform before
the Ark, initially with their backs to the congregation. Next, facing the
congregation, the priests raise their hands, fingers arranged in a special
way. At five different times while blessing the congregation they face
south and north, initially having faced east and finally facing the
congregation.

But none of this is observed because of a traditional rule that
priests and worshipers should *face* each other but must not *look* at each
other. Looking at each other is prohibited, according to the tradition, so
that the priests "not be distracted."[7] One is reminded of Freud sitting
behind his patient so that neither could see the other during the session.
Freud's arrangement has been explained: "To minimize *distraction* introduced by the reaction of the analyst and also to encourage relaxation
which fosters the free flow of thought, he [Freud] had the patient lie on
a couch and sat *out of his line of vision*" (emphasis added).[8] The Jewish
tradition and Freud give credence to each other's sense of a therapy
session.

There may be other reasons, too, that priests and congregation do
not look at each other during the Priestly Blessing. Since the worshiper
is reciting a prayer about dreams, which are visual, the averted eyes
serve to devalue the visual and thereby place high value on the aural –
the blessing. It is not insignificant, too, that the Priestly Blessing is

never recited at night, when normally one *sees* dreams, but in the daytime, when dreams have passed away and have lost at least some of their impact. Furthermore, the averted eyes serve to avoid a danger; for "objectivity emerges preeminently from sight . . . the sense of the passive observer par excellence."[9] The worshipers and priests, however, must not be passive observers. They are in an existential situation of intersubjectivity – God, the priests, and the worshipers responding to one another.

In the aural setting of the Priestly Blessing, the priests' arms and hands are extended, the fingers arranged fanlike – the thumb of each hand touching the other, and the first two fingers of each hand touching, separated from the other two touching fingers. The explanation for this is the traditional understanding of "He looketh in through the windows, He peereth through the lattice" (Songs of Songs 2:9), as referring to God, the Lover, looking at His people through the openings of the priests' hands. In this triadic situation of congregation, priests, and God, the only one who looks is the One who cannot be seen, cannot be distracted, and cannot be objectified.

The priests bless the congregation only on the five holidays during the year. Provision was made, therefore, for dealing with dreams throughout the year. This special service is known as the Amelioration of Dreams.[10]

Immediately after the weekday morning prayers a man who had a dream the previous night that "distressed" him gathers together, in the synagogue, three men who care about him,[11] from among his fellow worshipers. These three constitute a kind of court since in the Jewish tradition three laymen may constitute a court generally in civic matters.[12] Before these three men the dreamer declares, seven times, "I have seen a good dream." The Three respond, seven times, "You have seen a good dream. May the Merciful One overturn it unto the good; seven times may it be decreed by Heaven that it should be good and may it be good. It is good and it should be good."

Although the man had a dream that distressed him, his initial declaration is that his dream was good, an assertion insistently repeated by The Three. Yet both the dreamer and The Three know otherwise. No one is deceiving himself or the others. At issue is the traditional idea that "All dreams follow the mouth,"[13] that is, the interpretation. Both the dreamer and The Three, therefore, characterize the dream as good because they are not reporting the dream, which would be a kind of interpretation, but are interpreting it as having a good meaning. The dreamer does not tell his dream to The Three.[14] The liturgical direction is that the dreamer should "remember" the dream in his "thought" during this "time of the amelioration."

After these strained assertions about the dream being good, strained since the four men know otherwise, the dreamer prays, " 'Thou didst turn for me my mourning into dancing; thou didst loose my sackcloth and gird me with gladness' " (Psalm 30:12). The Three respond:

> "Then shall the virgin rejoice in the dance. And the young man and the old together, for I will turn their mourning into joy. And I will comfort them and make them rejoice from their sorrow" [Jeremiah 31:13]. "Nevertheless the Lord thy God would not hearken to Balaam, but the Lord thy God turned the curse into a blessing unto thee because the Lord thy God loved thee" [Deuteronomy 23:6].

These verses are recited, according to the Talmud, because each contains the word *overturn*,[15] since the dream, it is hoped, will be overturned from evil to the good.

The dreamer now says, " 'He hath redeemed my soul in peace so that none can come nigh me' " (Psalm 55:19), to which The Three respond:

> "And the redeemed of the Lord shall return and come with singing into Zion. And everlasting joy upon their heads; they shall obtain gladness and joy. And sorrow shall flee away" [Isaiah 35:10]. "And the people said unto Saul, Shall Jonathan die, who hath wrought this great salvation in Israel. Far from it, as the Lord liveth, there shall not one hair of his head fall to the ground, for he hath wrought with God this day. So the people redeemed Jonathan that he died not" [1 Samuel 14:45].

These verses are recited because each contains the word *redeem*; the dream is to be redeemed from evil to the good.[16]

The dreamer continues, " 'Peace, peace, to him that is far off and to him that is near, saith the Lord that createth the fruit of the lips; and I will heal him' " (Isaiah 57:19),[17] to which The Three respond:

> "Then the spirit clothed Amasai who was chief of the captains: Thine are we, David, and on thy side, thou son of Jesse. Peace, peace be unto thee, and peace be to thy helpers; for thy God helpeth thee. Then David received them and made them captain of the band" [1 Chronicles 12:19]. "And thus ye shall say: All hail! And peace be both unto thee, and peace be to thy house, and peace be unto all that thou hast" [1 Samuel 25:6]. "The Lord will give strength unto His people; the Lord will bless his people with peace" [Psalm 29:11].

These verses are recited because they contain the word *peace*.

The dreamer continues,[18] exclaiming three times, " 'O Lord, I have heard the report of Thee and am afraid,' " to which The Three respond with the rest of the verse, " 'O Lord, revive Thy work in the midst of the years; In the midst of the years make it known; In wrath remember compassion' " (Habakkuk 3:2).

The dreamer now says three times, " 'I will lift up my eyes unto the mountains: from whence shall my help come. My help cometh from the Lord, Who made heaven and earth.' " The Three respond with the rest of the psalm:

> "He will not suffer thy foot to be moved; He that keepeth thee will not slumber. Behold, He that keepeth Israel doth neither slumber nor sleep. The Lord is thy keeper. The Lord is thy shade upon thy right hand. The sun will not smite thee by day. Nor the moon by night. The Lord shall keep thee from all evil; He shall keep thy soul. The Lord shall guard thy going out and thy coming in from this time forth and forever" [Psalm 121:1–8].

The dreamer recites, " 'And the Lord spoke unto Moses, saying, Speak unto Aaron and his sons, saying, On this wise shall ye bless the children of Israel; ye shall say unto them.' " And The Three respond with the conclusion of this section of biblical passages: " 'The Lord bless thee and keep thee; the Lord make his face to shine upon thee, and be gracious unto thee; The Lord lift up his countenance upon thee and give thee peace' " (Numbers 6:22–26).

The dreamer now says, three times, " 'Thou makest me to know the path of life,' " to which The Three respond with the rest of the verse, " 'In thy presence is fullness of joy. In Thy right hand bliss for evermore' " (Psalm 16:11). And they add, " 'Go thy way, eat thy bread with joy. And drink thy wine with a merry heart. For God hath already accepted thy works' " (Ecclesiastes 9:7).

The dreamer makes a charitable contribution; and The Three respond with, " 'Repentance, prayer, and charity cancel the stern decree; Peace be on thee, on us, and on all Israel, Amen.' "[19]

The only references to the dream during the entire Amelioration of Dreams session are the initial declarations made by the dreamer and The Three.

The passages added to the Talmud's text[20] serve to make the session more effective therapeutically. The dreamer confesses to God that he is afraid and The Three respond with asking God to be compassionate. The selections from Psalms are both confessional and affirmative of God's providence. The Three, who are not priests, also recite the Priestly Blessing. The concluding verses about "path of life," "joy," "bliss," "go thy way," and "merry heart" serve to rid the dreamer of his despair. Significantly, although Ecclesiastes is quoted, its devaluation of dreams, "For a dream cometh through a multitude of business" (5:2), is not recited.

The recitation of the biblical verses by the dreamer and by The Three is, of course, in Hebrew. The verses are far less formal in Hebrew than in English translation. *Thy*, for example, has a stilted sound that the Hebrew second person singular pronoun does not have. Also important is the fact that the verses were, and are, rather well known and understood by the traditional Jew who attends synagogue services regularly.

The setting of the amelioration session is the synagogue, an environment formal and yet intimate. No directions are given as to how the session is to be conducted, the positions to be taken by the four men. The Codes make the point that the dreamer should choose three men that "love him." The codifiers, Jacob B. Asher (fourteenth century) and Joseph Caro (sixteenth century), must have had a good sense of the therapy aspect of the Amelioration of Dreams session, for as a modern therapist notes, "The success of all methods and schools of psychotherapy depends on the first instance in the patient's conviction that the therapist cares about him and is competent to help him."[21]

The session is, on the one hand, nothing other than a prayer service, the basic themes of which are change ("overturning"), redemption, and peace. There are no autobiographical statements made by the dreamer other than his first assertion. On the other hand, all of his biblical quotations are in a profound way autobiographical. Most of these texts from the sacred writings are an intimate part of these men's everyday life. The dreamer's first statement, "Thou didst turn for me my mourning into dancing, Thou didst loose my sackcloth and gird me with gladness" (Psalms 30:12), very familiar to the traditional Jew who recites it daily, is in this situation an autobiographical statement of hope, its first-person pronoun is not just the David of the psalm's rubric. The first-person pronoun in all the quotations is autobiographical. And the biblical texts with second- or third-person pronouns, other than those referring to God, recited by The Three, are, in this session, biographical of the dreamer.

This session of prayer is a therapy session not only because of its autobiographical and biographical statements but also, and perhaps primarily, because of its use of the blessing, an issue that we shall examine. As of now we note that the last declaration of the other three points up the therapeutic goal of the Amelioration of Dreams: "Go thy way, eat thy bread in joy. And drink thy wine with a merry heart. For God hath already accepted thy works" (Ecclesiastes 9:7). These words encourage him to overcome his distress, and his charitable act is the dreamer's first small step in the direction of his distress overcome.

There are differences and also similarities between the Priestly Blessing and the Amelioration of Dreams. For the latter, the dreamer asks three men who have no charisma, in the original meaning of this word, to help him deal with his distress. For the Priestly Blessing, the congregation, through the precentor, calls upon the priests who are divinely appointed, that is, who have the charisma, to bless the congregation during which time the prayer concerning dreams is recited. Although both take place in the synagogue, an institution laic yet holy, the setting of the Amelioration session is more intimate than that of the Priestly Blessing, which is conducted before an entire congregation during a formal service. Perhaps that is why there are very specific rules as to how the Priestly Blessing is to be conducted and no rules or directives about the setting of the Amelioration of Dreams session.

In both, the Priestly Blessing is recited, although in the Amelioration session it is not the only recitation by The Three as it is by the priests when they bless the congregation.

Both share something else. Just as the dreamer asks three men "who love him," as the directive notes, so, too, the priests respond to the precentor's summons with "and hast commanded us to bless His people Israel with love." For according to an old tradition a priest who does not love the congregation should not bless the people.[22] It is the biblically formulated blessing that gives them their therapeutic character.

In Jewish Scripture, a blessing is the "vital power without which no living being can exist . . . Blessing is life power . . . the power to live in its deepest and most comprehensive sense." Furthermore, "Wisdom is the same as blessing: the power to work and succeed . . . Understanding is the same as blessing, a power to live and accomplish the purpose that one has set for oneself in life."[23]

Modern students of therapy formulate a conception remarkably parallel to the biblical conception of blessing. According to Jerome D. Frank, "the goals of all forms of psychotherapy are to help the patient reduce or overcome his distress, to function better in his personal relationship and at work and concomitantly to increase his self esteem, and heighten his sense of control over himself and his surroundings."[24] According to Sheldon J. Korchin, "The therapeutic purpose involves increasing the patient's knowledge and capacity for effective life decisions."[25]

The wisdom and understanding, together with the peace and love, which the blessing gives is not a theoretical knowledge but an existential knowledge. What is sought during the Priestly Blessing and the Amelioration of Dreams service is not an interpretation of the dream but a *healing* of the dream and the dreamer's distress. For dream interpretation, according to the tradition, one goes to a dream interpreter. For healing of a dream, one stands before the priests during their "raising of the hands," to use the traditional term, as they bless the congregation; or one asks three friends, after the morning services, for dream amelioration. The words of Frieda Fromm-Reichmann can serve as a gloss to the controlling premise of traditional Jewish therapy: "The patient needs an experience, not an explanation."[26]

The experience during the Priestly Blessing and during the Amelioration of Dreams is, no doubt, different from the experience that Fromm-Reichmann had in mind. The latter is a secular experience; the former two are religious experiences. In these religious experiences the Therapist is ever present and always invisible and does not overtly respond as does a human therapist.

One might ask whether such therapy is effective. This is, of course, a relevant question about any kind of therapy, which can be answered only by a client and his therapist. In the religious therapeutic experience only the worshiper can testify to the effectiveness of the therapeutic experience.

Modern therapy and traditional Jewish therapy presuppose radically different assumptions. Modern therapy is naturalistic; God is the Absolute Irrelevancy in the therapeutic process. The social sciences, like the physical sciences, have no need for "theism." But for Jewish therapy, as for the entire Jewish tradition, God is always the One Who Is Present, as the tetragrammaton, the only name that is used in the Priestly Blessing recited in both services, signifies.[27]

Secular therapy and religious therapy, however, do presuppose the importance of *faith*. It is obvious that traditional Jewish dream therapy is based on faith in the Divine Therapist, Who responds to the prayer of the worshiper. For secular therapy, too, "Faith is important in different ways and at different times in psychotherapy. In the first instance the patient would not enter therapy without *belief* [my emphasis] in its curative powers nor, in the second, would he continue."[28] Obviously, the *content* of faith in these two different therapy structures is different.

The Priestly Blessing and the Amelioration of Dreams service are each, in a sense, "talking cures," as "Anna O." characterized modern therapy, and, like modern therapy, of some duration. The Priestly Blessing is conducted on five holidays during the Jewish liturgical year. All but one of these holidays are of more than one-day duration. Indeed, there can be (depending on different local customs) as many as thirteen recitations of the Priestly Blessing during the liturgical year. It was also a folk practice in some communities to recite the dream prayer during the precentor's daily oral recitation of the Eighteen Benedictions when he also recites the Priestly Blessing.[29]

The Amelioration of Dreams service could be performed as needed after the daily morning service (except Sabbath and holidays), and at least one authority was of the opinion that this service should be conducted after the daily evening service.

These two traditional dream therapy sessions are therefore of some duration during the course of the year.

Traditional Jewish dream therapy serves both men and women. While men and women in traditional synagogues are rigidly separated from each other, both attend the same services. The women also recite the prayer concerning dreams during the Priestly Blessing. As for the Amelioration of Dreams service, while the liturgical directives refer to the man, there is nothing prohibiting a woman who had a distressing dream from gathering three friends who "love" her and conducting that service. And women did, at least as late as the earlier decades of this century, attend daily morning synagogue services.

The Priestly Blessing service, with its prayer concerning dreams, is held in traditional synagogues in our time. The Amelioration of Dreams service is no longer in use since it has been deleted from current Orthodox editions of the traditional prayer book.

7

AMBIVALENCE

D reams are, as we have noted, of serious import in Jewish tradition. There is also, however, a disparagement of dreams.

The ambivalent attitude toward dreams is apparent in Hebrew Scripture, the primal text. For the traditional Jew, and those whose works we have discussed understood themselves as being traditional Jews, the different scriptural books were interrelated. There were, of course, the dreams of Joseph and Pharaoh, of Daniel and Nebuchadnezzar, and other biblical dreamers whose dreams were of significance. But there was the devaluation of dreams expressed by the wisest of men and kings, the "Solomon" of Ecclesiastes who, although in his dream (1 Kings 3:5-14) asked God for the wisdom, which he was granted, also expressed in Ecclesiastes his reservation about dreams, that they came with a "multitude of business" (5:2).

The Talmud, the primal hermeneutics of the primal text, also embodies this ambivalence. Tractate *Berakhot*, chapter 9, *Ha-Ro'eh* (One Who Sees), the locus classicus of rabbinic discussion of dreams, takes dreams seriously. Quoting many sages it contains a large number of interpretations of symbols seen in dreams. It also suggests some rules of dream interpretation. One of these rules has been discussed down the generations by rabbinic thinkers who concerned themselves with the interpretation of dreams: "All dreams follow the mouth." This apothegm was attributed to a Rabbi Bana'ah, a person of importance since he was the head of the Academy of Sepphoris. It was important enough to be transmitted by a group of rabbis: Bizna ben Zabda referred to this in the name of the very eminent Rabbi Akiva, who in turn had received it from Rabbi Panda, who had gotten it from Rabbi Nahum, who learned it from Rabbi Biryam, whose source was Rabbi Bana'ah.[1] Whether this rabbi was the one who first formulated this rule is not mentioned. Perhaps it was somewhat well known for there is a tantalizing reference to a book belonging to *the* dream interpreter Bar Hedya, which contained this very rule.[2]

The chapter "One Who Sees" contains the prayer about dreams that is recited during the Priestly Blessing and the Amelioration of Dreams prayer service. Since this chapter records the blessings that a person is to recite on seeing various things, it therefore includes the dreamer's response to his dreams, which are visual phenomena. This is the chapter that refers to Bar Hedya the dream interpreter. Bar Hedya expected to be paid for his services and therefore he might be considered by us to be a professional dream interpreter, although we are not informed as to his training. According to the Talmud, our only source, Bar Hedya gave a favorable interpretation of a dream to a client who compensated him; to a client who did not, Bar Hedya gave an unfavorable interpretation. Presumably the client who paid, paid in advance.

The Talmud recorded the experiences of two clients – Rava and Abaye.[3] These two eminent sages came to Bar Hedya for the interpretation of the thirteen dreams they had in common.[4] How it happened that these two sages, normally in opposition of one another in halakhic matters, had each the same dream, is not recorded.

Seven of these thirteen dreams were of biblical verses that both "had to recite" in their dreams. For each of these verses recited in the dreams Rava was given an unfavorable interpretation because he did not compensate Bar Hedya. Abaye, however, who did pay a *zuz*, apparently the standard fee (perhaps for each dream?), was given a favorable interpretation for each dream. Of the seven interpretations, the Talmud reports on the fulfillment of only one, that Rava was arrested on the suspicion of his breaking into the king's treasury, although, presumably, he was innocent.

These two sages also sought Bar Hedya's interpretation of the six other dreams in which each saw objects: lettuce on the mouth of a jar, meat on the mouth of a jar, a cask hanging from a palm tree, a pomegranate sprouting on the mouth of a jar, a cask falling into a pit, a young ass standing by the pillow and braying. For each similar dream, he gave Rava an unfavorable interpretation and Abaye a favorable one.

Subsequently Rava visited Bar Hedya without Abaye and recounted four dreams that Bar Hedya interpreted unfavorably. The result of only one is recorded. The dream of turnip tops meant two blows by a stick that Rava was to receive. The next day in the *Bet Midrash*, Rava, trying to separate two quarreling blind men, was attacked by them. After being hit twice he cried out, "Enough! I saw in my dream only two."

On another visit Rava paid Bar Hedya for interpreting five dreams, which were, therefore, interpreted favorably. Nothing is recorded, however, of the fulfillment of these favorable interpretations.

This rather lengthy section devoted to Bar Hedya and his interpretations begins with "Bar Hedya was an interpreter of dreams. To one who paid him he used to give a favorable interpretation and to one who did not pay him he gave an unfavorable interpretation."[5] It then presents the dreams of the two important clients of Bar Hedya and concludes with a final section about Bar Hedya and Rava.

They were both traveling by boat (nothing is said about the vessel or its destination), when Bar Hedya had misgivings about being on the same boat as Rava. Bar Hedya's fifth favorable interpretation of Rava's dream had been, "Miracles will happen to you," and that suddenly indicated to Bar Hedya that should an accident occur, only Rava, not he, would be saved. Bar Hedya, therefore, began to disembark. Rava noticed that a book that dropped as Bar Hedya was leaving had in it the aphorism "All dreams follow the mouth." Rava became angry; he now realized that his bad experiences were caused by Bar Hedya's unfavorable, because unpaid, interpretations, and not by the dreams. In his anger he called Bar Hedya wicked, accusing him, not the dreams, as the cause of his troubles.

Rava finally forgave him for all his troubles, except for the interpretation that caused the death of Rava's wife. For this interpretation Rava cursed Bar Hedya, that he be destroyed by the ruling power, that is, the Romans.

Fearing this sage's curse, Bar Hedya fled "to the Romans . . . and sat at the door of the keeper of the king's wardrobe," who asked Bar Hedya to interpret two dreams. Bar Hedya refused unless he was paid. The keeper in silence refused; then he told Bar Hedya of another dream, of a worm falling into his hand. Now Bar Hedya interpreted this dream as meaning that worms are devouring all the garments in the wardrobe. As this destruction became known in the royal menage it was decided that the keeper of the garments was to be executed for negligence. He protested his innocence, saying that it was Bar Hedya's negligence: "'He knew and would not tell.' So they brought Bar Hedya and they said to him: 'Because of your *zuz*, the king's silken garments have been ruined.' " And Bar Hedya was brutally executed.[6]

The Talmud's narrative about Bar Hedya and his two clients, Rava and Abaye, is not disinterested. It is derisive and full of mockery directed toward Bar Hedya the dream interpreter (who was also a sage). This is apparent, for instance, when Rava, in the academy on the day following the interpretation of a dream as meaning two blows, told the two blind men, "Enough! I saw in my dream only two," which lampoons Bar Hedya. Not only the criticism but the sarcasm is apparent in the Talmud's observation that Bar Hedya's interpretation was based on remuneration. Rava's calling Bar Hedya wicked and the denunciation by the gentile wardrobe keeper, "Because of your *zuz* the king's garments are ruined," also serve as the Talmud's criticism of Bar Hedya.

Bar Hedya is held in contempt because he interpreted for a price. He finally received his comeuppance because of the destruction he brought about when he did not receive a *zuz*.

In the first half of the thirteenth century, Meir ben Simeon Ha-Meili in his commentary to tractate *Berakhot* referred to Bar Hedya as "wicked," just as Rava had, and explained that he judged Bar Hedya as wicked because "for the sake of compensation he changes his word from good to evil."[7] This medieval commentator had a sense of the Talmud's disparagement of the one "professional" dream interpreter referred to in the Talmud. The section devoted to Bar Hedya embodies the Talmud's ambivalence about dreams and dream interpretation.

This ambivalence is also reflected in a statement that appears three times in the Talmud: "Dreams are of no consequence." In a situation of a person dreaming of a cache of money set aside for a second tithe, the sages said that "dreams are of no consequence."[8] When two sages dream that each is to go and reconcile with Rabbi Simeon ben Gamliel, only one of them, Rabbi Nathan, does so. Rabbi Meir, however, does not because he is of the opinion that "dreams are of no consequence."[9] In a case where a guardian of orphans was selling land and buying slaves, something forbidden by Rabbi Meir, Rabbi Meir ignored a dream challenging that ruling on the grounds that "dreams are of no consequence."[10]

These three references to sages denying the importance and validity of dreams counterbalance the significance attributed to dreams by many other sages, among whom were Abaye and Rava, in tractate *Berakhot*. Together they testify to the Talmud's ambivalence on the subject of dreams.

Ambivalence is apparent in posttalmudic traditional literature, the rabbinic works of the *Geonim*. Aaron Grünbaum summed it up: "In the geonic sources we do not find the ruling of the *Amelioration of Dreams* . . . In the works of the Geonim we do not have any statements about the dream interpretations that appear there [in *Berakhot*]."[11]

This silence of the *Geonim* about dreams in *Berakhot* also characterizes the medieval glossators of the Talmud, the Tosafists who are silent at the sections dealing with dreams, as well as the medieval codifiers. Of the latter, Grünbaum notes that two, Isaac ben Jacob Alfasi ("The Rif," 1013–1103) and Moses Maimonides (1135–1204), did not record the Amelioration of Dreams service. The ruling, however, that one who dreams of having been banned needs to be formally freed from that ban was recorded by the Geonim and Maimonides.[12]

The medieval commentators to the Talmud are also ambivalent on the subject of dreams. Menahem ben Solomon Meiri ("The Meiri," 1249–1316), Provencal scholar, in his commentary to tractate *Berakhot*, on the section devoted to chapter 9, transcribes the text of the Amelioration of Dreams with the suggestion that the three friends of the dreamer be told the dream so that they might interpret it. But, in any case, the service should be conducted. The prayer about dreams during the Priestly Blessing is also recorded by Meiri. This important commentator to the Talmud, however, has absolutely nothing to say about the many observations concerning dreams and their interpretations in this chapter of *Berakhot*.[13] He is studiously silent on the subject of dreams. He only felt obliged to record the therapy texts.

Simon ben Zemah Duran ("The Rashbatz," 1361–1441), born in Majorca, and after the massacre in 1391 left for Algiers, was an important rabbinic authority. Over eight hundred responsa of his have been recorded.[14] He was a physician and surgeon with philosophical and scientific interests.

In his responsa there are references to dreams. Dreams were evidently taken seriously in the Jewish community of Algiers. Questions were raised when some men had on different occasions dreamt that the community should fast in order to avert a disaster.[15] Duran also recorded a dream of his and his responsa to it. He dreamed one night that he had eaten nonkosher food; deeply disturbed, he awoke and recalled that the man who had delivered his meat the previous day had jocularly remarked, "Here is the meat prohibited and [then] permitted," and explained what he meant by this. Now Duran realized that this was what he ate in the dream. He then informed the delivery man that he wanted to have the meat returned and that this kind of meat should not be delivered to him again. While he as a rabbinic authority would not prohibit others from eating it, for himself it was not acceptable.[16]

Duran's *Magen Avot*[17] has, in the third section, seven and a half closely printed folio pages devoted to a wide-ranging philosophical-scientific analysis of dreams. Duran reflects on the nature of sleep and waking up, which leads him to a discussion of the senses, the humors, and digestion as factors in the phenomena of sleep and of dreaming. He presents six different topics for discussion on the nature of dreams. The first topic relates dreams to the "power of imagination" and the "power of memory." The second topic is the cause that makes for dreams. The third is why some dreams are valid, how this is possible, and of what class of knowledge they are, for example, the knowledge of the future that a dream might give must of necessity be of a "matter demarcated and in order [otherwise] . . . the active intellect has no knowledge of it."[18] The fourth topic deals with the fact that dreams are confined to sleep; the fifth, why some people have valid dreams and some have false dreams; and the sixth, why some people understand the interpretation of dreams while others do not.

The topics are discussed at great length with references to many thinkers. Of major importance for Duran was Aristotle, particularly what he thought was Aristotle's treatise *Ha-Shenah ve-ha-Yekizah* (Sleep and Awakening) which was probably Avicenna's work that had been translated from the Latin by Solomon ben Moses of Melgueuil some time in the thirteenth century.[19] Duran also refers to Aristotle's *Havayah ve-ha-Hefsed* (De Generatione et Corruptione), *Sefer ha-Hush ve-ha-Muhash* (De Sensu et Sensato), and *Ba'alei Hayyim* (De Animalibus). He mentions Galen a number of times; most frequently he refers to Ibn Roshd (Averroes), once to Ibn Sina (Avicenna), and once to astronomers. Of Jewish thinkers he refers to Maimonides, particularly *The Guide*, to Abraham Ibn Ezra, and to Gersonides whom he cites frequently, particularly *The Wars of the Lord* and Gersonides' abridgement of Aristotle's *De Sensu et Sensato*.

Duran quotes a number of the Talmud's observations about dreams: Bar Hedya's interpretations and other statements in *Berakhot*, and references to dream interpretation in *Lamentations Rabbah* and in tractate *Second Tithes* of Talmud Jerusalem. But these are cited as exemplifying philosophic-scientific truth. The rabbinic aphorisms and meanings of symbols do not serve Duran in his analysis of dreams.

Two incidents that he records, all too tantalizingly briefly, deserve mention since they note medieval Jewish folk practice. Duran records that his father told him that his [Simon's] paternal great-grandfather had "elicited a dream and had been vouchsafed true matters on awakening." And, Duran adds, "we have seen many incidents, even among our women, [in which] things were seen [presumably in dreams] which troubled them; and that which they saw, so it [*sic*] came about completely."[20] Duran did not record his response to these two different experiences, but the fact that he recorded them would indicate that he considered them important.

Because Duran as a devout Jew and as a jurist had to confront the meaning of dreams and as a philosopher-scientist wanted to account for the phenomenon of dreams, it is surprising that in his commentary to tractate *Berakhot*[21] he does not make a single comment on the dream material in chapter 9 of *Berakhot*. Perhaps Duran revealed here not his ambivalence about dreams but his ambivalence about the Talmud's observations on the subject of dreams.

Ambivalence about dreams is also expressed during the waning of the Middle Ages by Hayyim Vital (1542–1620), one of the important Safed kabbalists. In his *Book of Visions*,[22] a diary of his dreams and the dreams of others about him, an unabashedly egocentric volume that records his certainty of his greatness, he felt that he had to justify composing a book that recorded dreams. He therefore wrote, "Do not wonder that I write down dreams," and he justifies his enterprise by quoting the *Midrash to Ecclesiastes*, tractate *Berakhot's* references to Rava–Abaye–Bar Hedya, along with a few other similar references. But these references do not validate the composing of a dream diary.[23] That Vital had to justify this diary reveals his uncertainty and the ambivalence toward dreams current in a traditional Jewish community.

Ambivalence also characterizes traditional Jewish scholarship in the twentieth century. In the learned Orthodox Hebrew journal *Shevilin*,[24] Rabbi Ch. D. Halevi published "The Raising of the Hands," a fourteen-page study of the Priestly Blessing. He discusses the presuppositions of this blessing, the rules and the process, and so forth, of the blessing. Two pages at the very end contain 160 footnotes. The last section of the study, only a page and a quarter, is devoted to the dream prayer recited during the Priestly Blessing. Rabbi Halevi entitled this section "The Dream and Its Interpretation," a curious title when one reflects on the Hebrew word, which I have correctly translated as *interpretation*. The Hebrew word is *sever*. Now this word for interpretation is found only once in all of Hebrew Scripture, in Judges 7:15: "And it was so, when Gideon heard the telling of the dream and the *interpretation*," and is never used for interpretation in the Talmud.[25] It was practically never used for interpretation in medieval Jewish literature.[26] Whether such a rare word for interpretation was intentionally or accidentally chosen by him I do not know. But since a homonym of that word means *break*, I surmise that Rabbi Halevi consciously chose this rarely used word for *interpretation* in order to derogate the importance of dreams.

This, in fact, is the thrust of the last section of the article. With a melange of passages from Scriptures, Talmud, and medieval texts, he tries to temper the importance of dreams in human life. And Rabbi Halevi concludes this section of his study with a one-sentence paragraph:

> Happy is the man who is healthy in intellect and spirit, who, because of his great reliance on God, does not fear or tremble and who fulfills for himself 'Thou shalt be whole-hearted with the Lord thy God' [Deuteronomy 18:13], and the Lord will not withhold the good from those who walk whole-heartedly; Happy is the man who relies on the Lord, and the Lord is his Reliance.

It is obvious that while nothing in the article tends to devaluate the importance of the Priestly Blessing, the section devoted to the dream prayer, recited twice during the blessing, serves to dismiss the prayer.

Ambivalence is also apparent in the contemporary orthodox *Encyclopedia Talmudit*. This impressively learned work, as yet very far from being complete, characterizes itself as dealing with *halakhah*. Its article, "The Matter of Dreams,"[27] consisting of four and a half pages of text and detailed footnotes, is divided into four sections. The first section, "Dreams in General," starts with denial – "Dreams are of no consequence"[28] – and it reiterates this, as we shall note, although it also says that there are many "valid dreams" and that many postbiblical sages had explained that there were prophetic dreams. But the sages also said that one is shown in dreams only what one thinks during the day. The rest of this first section continues in this vein and concludes:

> There are those who have written, and it is a well known matter and the whole world knows, that most dreams, and the vast majority, are all empty things and lies and vanities and do not contain even one thing that is true. For it "cometh with a multitude of business" and much imagination. Or by means of the vapors that arise from the stomach as the naturalists [i.e., the scientists] have said; for even the true dreams that come through prophecy or intelligence, they all contain a bit of meaningless things.[29]

The three legal issues of the article are addressed after the initial disparagement: (1) should one rely on the verity of what is revealed to a dreamer about what was previously unknown to him; (2) should a man act in response to being banned in a dream, that is, retribution dreamed about; (3) should a man take seriously an obligation taken upon himself while dreaming?

The first of these is discussed in terms of specific legal issues and resolved with the assurance that dreams are not serious, with the added statement, quoted five times, that "dreams are of no consequence." The last paragraph in this topic reads:

> As for the revealing of hidden things [in a dream], on the matter of clarifying uncertainty about halakhah by means of a dream, many early authorities did depend on dreams; and they taught an halakhah or reversed their earlier teachings on the basis of what appeared to them in a dream [an extensive footnote giving references accompanies this point]. These were those who elicited dreams [to resolve their uncertainties]. Among the early authorities there were those who wrote that among the *Amoraim* there were those who elicited dreams. In any case the jurists wrote that in this matter, too, it is said, "Dreams are of no consequence" and one does not rely on such.[30]

The second topic, dreaming of being banned, states that one has to be freed formally from the ban because "a dream is a kind of prophecy . . . and their saying of 'dreams are of no consequence' did not mean to deny its [the dream's] strength." The issue is discussed at length with many footnotes of attribution. The legal procedure of lifting the ban is described at length.

The third topic, obligations that a dreamer takes upon himself, for example, taking a vow or an oath, is dealt with by presenting different legal opinions. The issue is taken seriously.

This article, "The Matter of Dreams," fully documented with 128 footnotes, is ambivalent. It begins with disparaging its subject matter, which is surprising since the *Encyclopedia Talmudit*, committed to traditional Judaism, is written in a disinterested manner. The authors, a group of learned men, forgo taking sides in any dispute about legal matters. Each article sums up the different views on each issue.

That this article begins with a disparagement that it quotes four more times, inter alia, though this was not necessary, raises the question as to whether or not the anonymous author wanted, perhaps unconsciously, to discourage one from reading the article. Furthermore, the author may have been out of bounds; for this disparagement, the source of which is the Talmud, is not halakhic, yet the *Encyclopedia Talmudit* proclaims its halakhic orientation.

Since this author writes a nonlegal introduction on the matter of dreams in this twentieth century, when dreams have been explored once again with renewed vigor, so that it is no longer a neglected language, it is naive of him to dismiss it so easily. A much earlier jurist, Duran, whom our author quotes nine times,[31] did reflect on the nature of dreams, although, as we pointed out, he was ambivalent. He had read Jewish thinkers and gentile philosophers on the subject of dreams. The anonymous author of this encyclopedia article, in his introduction, evinces no awareness of twentieth-century studies of dreams.

In the *Encyclopedia Talmudit*'s entry "The Amelioration of Dreams,"[32] there is transcribed both the service and the directions for conducting it, after which the anonymous author states that according to later authorities, a person should accustom himself not to take dreams seriously, since they are of no value. They come with a "multitude of business" (Ecclesiastes 5:2), resulting from the thoughts and interests of the day.

Also included in this article is the prayer concerning dreams recited during the Priestly Blessing. It suggests that should there be no priests to recite the blessing the worshipers may recite the dream prayer during the precentor's recitation of the prayer of the Eighteen Benedictions, at one or another specific point in that recitation. This author does not disparage dreams. His reference to what later authorities said serves only to temper the importance of dreams.

The *Encyclopedia Talmudit* and the journal *Shevilin*, in publishing Rabbi Ch. D. Halevi's study of the Priestly Blessing, unintentionally call attention to ambivalence on the subject of dreams, at least among some of the learned circles within contemporary Orthodox Jewry.

8

THE FOUR DREAM INTERPRETERS

Three of the four dream interpreters, Bar Hedya, Solomon Almoli, and Judah Ftayya, each from a different era, were men learned in the rabbinic traditions.

Bar Hedya is something of an enigma because we know of him only from the Talmud where, aside from tractate *Berakhot*, he is referred to only six times and, at that, only in passing.[1] He was an *amora*, one of the postmishnaic sages and, therefore, a learned man. We do not know how he became a dream interpreter, whether he received formal training or was an autodidact with a natural flair or aptitude for dream interpretation. The book he had with him on his trip, which had at least one reference to dreams, might have been composed by him, but we do not know.

Bar Hedya was a professional dream interpreter, interpreting dreams according to compensation. The Talmud, in tractate *Berakhot*, with its account of his just desserts, is not favorably disposed toward him. Bar Hedya took his interpretation of dreams seriously; he left the boat on which Rava was also traveling, convinced that his interpretation of Rava's dream excluded him from being saved.

Solomon Almoli, at the waning of the Middle Ages, was a very different kind of dream interpreter. We know considerably more about him than we know about Bar Hedya, but we know very little about his daily life. He was a physician and his patients may have told him their dreams, seeking his interpretations. He was aware of people's needs and was concerned about them, for he permitted his *Interpretation of Dreams* to circulate before he decided to have it published. Perhaps he wrote this book as a result of his experiences as a physician who was concerned about his patients.

Almoli earned a living by his medical practice, having become a physician in order to support his family. Almoli was a rabbi and a member of the Jewish court of Constantinople; he was, therefore, trained in traditional Jewish scholarship. He believed that an earlier Jewish discipline of dream interpretation should be revitalized, that originally there had been practitioners of that discipline.

Almoli felt isolated and ignored by his colleagues. He was rather bitter. He had much knowledge that he wanted to share with others but was not given the opportunity to do so.[2] Perhaps these were factors in his decision to write *Interpretation of Dreams*. Almoli succeeded to an extent that he could not have foreseen. His book became the most important work on dream interpretation in the traditional Jewish community.

Judah Ftayya, a not-too-distant contemporary of ours, was a different kind of person from both Bar Hedya and Solomon Almoli. He was an ebullient man, very involved with people. He would sit in front of his house in Baghdad and greet people, comforting them with his blessings and advising them. He served as a therapist for people who had been invaded by a dybbuk. He interpreted dreams for all kinds of people, for scholars, for young students, for blue-collar workers, both men and women. He was also a traditional Jewish academician. In the evening at different institutions in Baghdad, one of which he founded, he taught Talmud and Kabbalah to businessmen, some very wealthy, who were also learned in the traditional Jewish texts. By day Ftayya taught Talmud to the youth of Baghdad. As an ordained rabbi he was also a member of the Jewish court in Baghdad.

Ftayya may have received fees for his interpretations of dreams; we do not know. Only one fleeting reference, not in connection with dreams, however, may indicate that he was compensated.[3] One can assume that he earned his living as a member of the court and as an instructor in traditional academic institutions.

These three interpreters of dreams were not ambivalent about the importance of dreams or the validity of dream interpretation. The three were deeply involved with rabbinic traditions, although Bar Hedya who flourished during the second stage of its development did not encounter its subsequent richness.

Almoli and Ftayya share something else that Bar Hedya, of necessity, could not know. Almoli and Ftayya were both kabbalists. Almoli only indicates this by his frequent references to the *Zohar* and by his kabbalistic hints en passant. In Ftayya, Kabbalah is explicit; it is important in his thinking, in his piety, in his own dreams, and in his interpretation of the dreams of others.

To a greater or lesser degree these three share a major enterprise – hermeneutics. Bar Hedya interpreted the dreams of recitation of biblical verses by Abaye and Rava. Bar Hedya's education, we can be sure, included a close knowledge of the biblical texts and the developing traditional hermeneutics. Almoli and Ftayya knew not only the biblical texts but the fully developed rabbinic traditional hermeneutics that they mastered.

Almoli and Ftayya, and Bar Hedya, too, in all probability, did not study dreams; they studied books, biblical-rabbinic works, and medieval commentaries about dreams. Almoli was a grammarian and studied poetry. Language was one of his fortes. It is not insignificant that Ftayya discusses dreams, his dreams and their meanings, and clients' dreams and his interpretations of them in his book devoted to biblical hermeneutics.

It is striking that three of these interpreters of dreams were jurists. Bar Hedya was one of the *amoraim* and among "their tasks, [one] was to derive conclusions from the halakhah in the Mishnah and other tannaitic collections,"[4] which means that Bar Hedya was involved with hermeneutics.

Almoli and Ftayya as members of the Jewish court in their respective cities were also involved with the interpretation of legal texts. And Ftayya, who composed a hefty commentary to a kabbalistic work by Vital, was a teacher of Talmud texts, texts closely read and explicated.

These three men, close students of legal texts and devotional, for example, biblical, texts and commentaries, given to analyzing language, both legal and nonlegal, were, therefore, not surprisingly, also adept at the language of dreams.

A. B. was a twentieth-century oneirocritic writer in America. An East European Jew, as indicated by his rich Yiddish vocabulary, A. B. is something of an enigma because we do not know his name or what his occupation was. He was distinctively different from the other three dream interpreters, including Ftayya who was also a twentieth-century Jew.

A. B. was learned in traditional texts, although in all probability not as learned as the others. He may have studied in a *yeshivah* before he came to America. But if he did, he rejected traditional Judaism, so much so that the few biblical references in his book refer to the dreams of two gentile kings, not to Israelite kings, and to two gentile commoners, not to Israelite commoners, except for Joseph, whose dreams he deliberately misinterpreted. Although he quotes the Talmud's apothegm "All dreams follow the mouth," A. B. asserts the validity of it by virtue of an account of a gentile oneirocritic's successful interpretation of a dream and subsequent reflections on the interpretation. Another talmudic statement, "A wise man is even superior to a prophet," is used by him to undercut the traditional belief in prophecy, which the Talmud did not do by this statement.

For the other three interpreters, biblical hermeneutics was most important in dream interpretation. Biblical verses, particularly assonance, served to interpret dreams. The importance of the Word in traditional dream interpretation was ignored by A. B.

Ftayya and A. B. do, however, share something. They both deal with sexuality in the dreams of their contemporaries; and they both, Ftayya for his clients and A. B. through his book, interpret women's dreams. Furthermore, both are not conventionally traditional. This is obvious in A. B. but not in Ftayya. Ftayya, as we noted, dreamed of Nathan of Gaza and Shabbetai Zevi. He was clearly sympathetic to them, each of whom was a persona non grata in the orthodox community. This sympathy for what by the twentieth century was at best fragments of a submerged heretical piety is characteristic of Ftayya's individualistic modernity.

The anonymous author of the "The Matter of Dreams" in the *Encyclopedia Talmudit*, also trained in the Jewish juridical tradition, views dreams very differently from Bar Hedya, Solomon Almoli, Judah Ftayya, and A. B. In his short article he reiterates the Talmud's "Dreams are of no consequence." Bar Hedya, Abaye, and Rava, who consulted him, and the many others in tractate *Berakhot* who sought interpretation for their dreams, and Almoli, A. B., and Ftayya did not denigrate dreams. What transpired in the Jewish tradition that made for the *Encyclopedia Talmudit*'s belittling of dreams and the Halevi article's dismissal of the prayer about dreams?

Something did occur in the rabbinic tradition that accounts for it. The encyclopedia's self-definition proclaims this. Under its title *Encyclopedia Talmudit* there are the Hebrew words, *"L'inyenei Halakhah"* ("Concerning Issues of Halakhah"), which implies that it circumvents all the aggadic material that is also part of the Talmud. What occurred was what might be termed a postclassical Jewish rationalism. There are strains of this in geonic and postgeonic literature. Some of the Geonim and medieval talmudists were embarrassed by the rabbinic *aggadot*. Twentieth-century halakhists tend to ignore *aggadah*.

This rationalism is reflected in the prayer books used in the synagogues. The traditional prayer book published by the orthodox Mesorah Publications, *The ArtScroll Siddur*,[5] "a new translation and anthologized commentary" by Rabbi Nosson Scherman, does include the prayer concerning dreams recited during the Priestly Blessing, with the following footnote:

> During sleep the soul divests itself of the corporeal garb which inhibits its free movement during the day. Thus, in his dreams, one is able to soar above his body and attain the higher spiritual forces of eternal life, yet upon awakening he will be unaware of the implications of what he has attained [attributed to *Maggid Mesharim*, presumably by Joseph Caro].[6]

But this rather comprehensive prayer book does not include the Amelioration of Dreams service.

The prayer book of Conservative Judaism, *Siddur Sim Shalom*,[7] contains the Priestly Blessing with the introductory note "In congregations where the kohanim [i.e., priests] chant the blessings the Reader continues here"[8] and the blessing is transcribed; but the prayer concerning dreams is deleted. The Amelioration of Dreams service is, of course, not included in this prayer book.

The prayer book of Reform Judaism, *Gates of Prayer: The New Union Prayerbook*,[9] deletes the prayer concerning dreams as it deletes the Priestly Blessing service and it does not contain the Amelioration of Dreams service.

Judah Ftayya and A. B. may have been the last of the Jewish oneirocritics serving just their own Jewish communities. Ftayya, devout jurist and kabbalist of heretical sympathies, and A. B., staunch secular-ethnic Jew, unlike contemporary halakhists and modern traditional and nontraditional prayer books, maintain a traditional concern for people troubled by their enigmatic experiences during sleep time.

NOTES

INTRODUCTION

1. Ken Frieden, *Freud's Dream of Interpretation* (Albany, NY: State University of New York Press, 1990), pp. 2, 17–18, 54.
2. *Perush Al Ha-Torah*, vol. 1 (Jerusalem: Bnai Arbel, 1963), p. 386. My translation.

CHAPTER 1

1. *Berakhot* 57b. The passage adds that "a dream is a sixtieth of prophecy."
2. V. Aubert and H. White, "Sleep, A Sociological Interpretation," in *Sociology and Every Day Life*, ed. M. Truzzi (Englewood Cliffs, NJ: Prentice-Hall, 1968), p. 135.
3. Erwin Straus, *The Primary World of the Senses* (New York: Free Press of Glencoe, 1963), p. 275.
4. Cf. Alexander Kristianpoller, "Traum und Traumdeutung," in *Monumenta Talmudica* (Vienna: Harz, 1923), vol. 4, part 2, transcribed 216 passages from the Talmud and other rabbinic works dealing with dreams. He added comprehensive footnotes.

5. Daniel, chaps. 2, 4, 7.

6. We have given only a few references to dreams in Hebrew Scripture. For a comprehensive study, cf. Shaul Bar, "Dreams in the Bible" (Ph.D. diss., New York University, 1987; UMI Dissertation Service, Ann Arbor, MI).

7. *Berakhot* 20a, 35b, 55a, 63a.

8. *Berakhot* 14a. Soncino translation will be used throughout unless otherwise designated.

9. *Berakhot* 55a.

10. Ibid. Deduced from Genesis 37:9.

11. Ibid.

12. See chapter 6, "Dream Therapy in Jewish Tradition."

13. *Berakhot* 55b. In the Palestinian Talmud a somewhat different text is recorded that is not noted as recited during the Priestly Blessing. Curiously, there is no reference to Joseph's dream in the Palestinian version. Cf. *Berakhot*, Yerushalmi (Bnai Brak, 1980), vol. 1, part 1.

14. *Berakhot* 55b.

15. Ibid.

16. *Lamentations Rabbah*, chap. 1, paragraph (hereafter shown as ¶) 2, Soncino translation, pp. 69–70.

17. Not all that follows in the chapter will be referred to. The important material on Bar Hedya and his two clients will be discussed in chapter 7, "Ambivalence."

18. *Berakhot* 56b.

19. Soncino *Berakhot* simply transliterates *Min* (p. 346). The Steinsaltz edition has the Hebrew *Min*, the standard Hebrew texts have *Zadoki*, i.e., *Sadducean*. Cf. *Encylopaedia Judaica*, vol. 12, cols. 1–3, *Min*.

20. R. Ishmael's statement, after the man said that his father had not gone to Cappadocia, was: "In that case *kappa* means *beam*; *dike* means *ten*. Go and examine the beam which is at the head of ten for it is full of coins." The Soncino translation, p. 347, includes a footnote explaining that the word for *beam* is Aramaic and the word for *ten* is a Greek word. Cf. also Rashi, ad loc.

21. Ibid., the very last phrase is Soncino's translation.

22. Ibid.; cf. Soncino, p. 48 n. 2.

23. Ibid.

24. *Berakhot* 56b–57a.

25. *Berakhot* 57a.

26. Ibid.

27. Ibid.

28. *Berakhot* 57b.

29. *Berakhot* 57a. My translation.

30. *Ketubot* 110b.

31. Saul Lieberman, *Hellenism in Jewish Palestine* (New York: Jewish Theological Seminary, 1950), p. 52.

32. This anonymous midrash is found in *Midrash Ha-gadol Bereshit*, ed. M. Margulies (Jerusalem: Mosad Ha-Rav Kook, 1947), p. 39. The translation I have used is that by Saul Lieberman, op. cit., p. 70. On p. 71 he refers to a study by H. Lewy that "demonstrated the close parallel between Artemidoros' *Onirocriticon* and the dream interpretation of the Rabbis." This study in *Rheinisches Museum f. Philologie*, N.F. 48 (1893), pp. 398–419, is unavailable to me.

33. *Pirkey Avot* 5:22. The translation is by Danby. Cf. *The Mishnah*, trans. Herbert Danby (Oxford: Clarendon Press, 1933), p. 438.

34. *Amos* 8:1–2.

35. Johannes Pedersen, *Israel: Its Life and Culture*, vol. 1 (London: Oxford University Press; Copenhagen: Pavel Branner, 1946 reprint), pp. 167–168.

36. A. Leo Oppenheim, *The Interpretation of Dreams in the Ancient Near East* (Transactions of the American Philosophical Society, vol. 46/3; Philadelphia: American Philosophical Society, 1956), pp. 236–237.

37. Genesis 37:18–19.

38. I rely on Ch. J. Kasowski, *Otzar L'shon Ha-Talmud*, vol. 8 (Jerusalem: The Government of the State of Israel and The Jewish Theological Seminary of America, 1959), p. 694.

39. *Sanhedrin* 30a, p. 83, modified. The Soncino translator, in n. 8, gives as an alternative to his "dispenser of dreams," the "master of dreams" and adds, "which merely [*sic*] represents the personification of the dream."

40. *Berakhot* 10b, modified. Cf. Soncino n. 6 on the translation of Ecclesiastes 5:6.

41. *The Tosefta*, vol. 1, *Zeraim*, ed. Saul Lieberman (New York: The Lewis Rabinowitz Research Institute in Rabbinics, The Jewish Theological Seminary of America, 1955), "Masser Sheni," p. 270. My translation. In n. 31 Lieberman explains *Ish halom* as *Sar ha-halomot*; he may have disdained the term *ba'al ha-halom*.

42. *Avot d' Rabbi Nathan*, ed. S. Schechter, corrected 3rd ed. (New York/Philadelphia: Feldheim, 1967), p. 66.

43. *Midrash Tannaim al Sefer Devarim*, ed. Z. Hoffman (Berlin: Z. H. Itzkowski, 1908–1909), p. 199.

44. *Midrash Shir Ha-Shirim*, ed. Joseph Chaim Wertheimer (Jerusalem: Ktav Yad Va-Sefer, 1971), pp. 61–62. This midrash "was apparently redacted in the eleventh century." Cf. *Enc. Jud.*, vol. 16, col. 1515.

45. *Midrash Ha-Gadol, Exodus*, ed. Mordecai Margolis (Jerusalem: Mosad Ha-Rav Kook, 1956), p. 375. This thirteenth-century rabbinic commentary composed in Yemen is for the most part made up of earlier rabbinic texts. Popular in the Yeminite community even in relatively recent times, cf. *Enc. Jud.*, vol. 11, cols. 1515–1516.

46. *Sefer Hasidim*, ed. Jehuda Wistinetzki and Jacob Freimann, 2nd ed. (Jerusalem: Wahrmann Books, 1969), p. 102, ¶324, and p. 373, ¶1521.

47. Solomon Almoli, *Pitron Halomot* (Warsaw: Lewin-Epstein, 1902), p. 22.

CHAPTER 2

1. *The Romance of the Rose*, trans. H. W. Robbins (New York: E. P. Dutton, 1962), p. 3.

2. *Sefer Mitzvot Gadol* (Venice, 1547), vol. 1, Introduction, p. 3A (reprinted in Israel, 1961). My translation throughout.

3. I am intentionally substituting "polis dream" for "political dream," the usual way of referring to this unusual phenomenon since the term *political* has too many other connotations.

4. *Sefer Mitzvot Gadol*, vol. 2 (Munkacs, 1905), p. 3B.

5. *Sh'ailot uT'Shuvot min Ha-shamayim*, ed. Reuben Margulies (Jerusalem: Mosad Ha-Rav Kook, 1957).

6. Cf. ibid., p. 22, Introduction.

7. The most frequent formula is "I asked"; for these dreams came to R. Jacob not in a haphazard way but as a result of questions that he presented. The "I asked" is the rubric for the question, and the rubric for the dream as recorded by R. Jacob is "they answered." On occasion this is varied, for example, "after an hour they answered" (¶50, p. 73). The meaning of "they" is found in ¶3 (p. 44), which is concerned with a legal nicety on a question dealing with phylacteries: "And this was my question: O, the Great, Mighty, Awesome King, Knower of secrets, Revealer of secrets, Teller of hidden things, Guardian of the covenant and *hesed*, magnify

your *hesed* to us this very day. Command your holy angels to inform me . . . [on the matter of phylacteries]. . . . And now King of kings, command your holy angels to inform me as to . . . the law." After this question, which is a prayer addressed to God to the effect that His angels be instructed to answer, the answer is immediately introduced by "they answered." So, too, in ¶5 where R. Jacob presents a question and the second recorded answer is introduced by the rubric "after this they answered, 'we have from behind the curtain. . . .' "

Clearly, then, "they" refers to the angels. ¶3 seems to indicate that his way of presenting his question was through prayer. It may very well be, however, that the prayer was recited within the dream and was not the technique of presenting the question. R. Jacob elicited the dream answer through a very definite technique. He seems to have written out his question and (perhaps) placed the question near him while he slept. The answer was found written when he awoke (no doubt this was due to automatic writing).

Our assumption as to technique is based on the following: ¶8, p. 53, recording two answers, concludes, "All this they answered me in the order I had written"; ¶56, p. 75, records the following answer, "Not on the basis of wisdom did you ask such a question . . . 'Have I not written unto thee excellent things of counsels.' " The quotation within the dream is a direct quotation from Proverbs 22:20 but this does not detract from the significant "I have written." This verse was chosen because of its specific relevancy. It clearly indicates that the answers received were written answers. Further evidence of this is found in the terse ¶72, p. 80: "And concerning the time of [messianic] redemption he also asked but he did not find a written answer before him." Undoubtedly this was recorded by another person but the other person certainly knew how the answers were received.

It seems that it did not necessarily take a full night's sleep to receive an answer. While he frequently makes no reference to time, when he does R. Jacob indicates that it took *sha'ah ahat*, which, of course, does not necessarily mean a sixty-minute hour. On occasion, two *sha'ot* pass before an answer is received. In one instance, R. Jacob did not understand the answer; therefore, "on the second night I repeated [the question] and I asked that the answer be explained to me or that another, clearer answer be given. They answered me as in the first instance, and [then] they explained" (¶32, p. 67).

8. *Sh'ailot uT'Shuvot min Ha-Shamayim*, ¶5, p. 52.

9. Ibid., ¶22, pp. 61–62.

10. This study is based on the Parma MS of *Sefer Hasidim*, ed. J. Wistinetzki and J. Freimann (Frankfort am Main, 1924) and on the Bologna MS, ed. R. Margulies (Jerusalem: Mosad Ha-Rav Kook, 1957); the latter will be specified when quoted.

11. *Sefer Hasidim*, ¶271, p. 86.

12. Ibid., ¶63, p. 48.

13. Cf. Oppenheim, *The Interpretation of Dreams in the Ancient Near East*, p. 226. Despite obviously vast differences between the ancient Near East and thirteenth-century Germany there are significant parallels that validate our use of this work. Furthermore, and what is equally important, Oppenheim's work enables the modern scholar to come to grips more readily with the medieval material for it makes it possible to look beyond the modern psychoanalytic assumptions that permeate all of our thinking. A judicious use of this work contributes much to one's understanding. It seems that very little *historical* work has been done on the subject of dreams. Oppenheim's work, therefore, serves as a control and as a source of insight.

14. *Sefer Hasidim*, ¶324, p. 102

15. Both MSS have *adam qatan*, which does not make sense. I am adopting the reading proposed by Margulies, op. cit., in his commentary *maqor hesed* ad loc., ¶441, p. 304.

16. *Sefer Hasidim*, ¶382, pp. 116–117.

17. Gershom Scholem, *Major Trends in Jewish Mysticism* (Jerusalem: Schocken, 1941), p. 79.

18. *Sefer Hasidim*, ¶384, p. 117.

19. ¶1522, p. 373

20. ¶383, p. 117.

21. ¶1563, p. 382.

22. ¶180, p. 72. Cf. Margulies' commentary to the Bologna MS op. cit., ¶684, p. 431, for some suggestions as to the relevancy of the symbol.

23. *Sefer Hasidim*, ¶266, p. 86.

24. ¶1525, pp. 373–374.

25. ¶1523, p. 373. The references to the animals in the dream are unclear in the Hebrew text.

26. ¶389, p. 118.

27. Op. cit., p. 207.

28. Ibid., pp. 218, 219.
29. ¶281, p. 90.
30. Op. cit., p. 219.
31. Ibid.
32. Op. cit., p. 220.
33. ¶388, p. 118.
34. ¶389, p. 118.
35. ¶1138, p. 288.
36. Cf. Oppenheim, op. cit., p. 232.
37. Ibid., p. 236f.
38. ¶382, p. 116; ¶384, p. 117.
39. ¶382, p. 116; ¶1451, p. 353.
40. ¶324, p. 102; ¶1521, pp. 372–373; and perhaps ¶1550, p. 380 where the ambiguous term *the appointed one* is used.
41. ¶1521, pp. 372–373.
42. ¶322, p. 101.
43. ¶80, p. 53.
44. ¶1556, p. 381.
45. ¶1456, p. 353.
46. ¶324, p. 102.
47. ¶266, p. 86.
48. Cf. Oppenheim, op. cit., p. 209, for a discussion on "political" dreams.
49. ¶265, p. 86.
50. ¶321, p. 101. Wistinetzki's suggestions, n., ad loc., to delete three words is doubtful. *Hayu* changed to *hayah* maintains the text and makes sense. For the full understanding of the premises of the dream, A. Price's gloss is most helpful, cf. his *Mishnat Avraham*, a commentary to *Sefer Hasidim* (Toronto: G. Shepard, 1955), vol. 1, ad loc.
51. ¶323, p. 101.
52. ¶264, p. 86.
53. ¶1530, p. 375. Wistinetzki's emendation, ad loc., is not necessary, it seems to me.
54. ¶269, p. 86.
55. Cf. ¶375, p. 114, where a young man dies in the place of his teacher; we have not quoted this in our study.

56. ¶386, p. 118.

57. ¶325, p. 102.

58. ¶390, p. 118.

59. Cf. n. 18.

60. ¶385, p. 117.

CHAPTER 3

1. Bibliographical and biographical data are from H. Yalon's "Afterword" to his edition of Almoli's grammatical work *Helikhot Sheva* (Jerusalem, 1944), pp. 79–115; from Yalon's study, "Chapters from R. Solomon Almoli's Me'asseph le-Khol ha Mahanoth" in *Areshet*, vol. 2 (Jerusalem, 1960), pp. 96–108 (reprinted with additions in Yalon's *Pirkey Lashon*, Jerusalem, 1971, pp. 218-232); and from A. Grünbaum's study "Pitron Halomot: History and Sources" in *Areshet*, vol. 4 (Jerusalem, 1966), pp. 180-201. Freud referred to Almoli in *Die Traumdeutung* in a footnote on page 3, "Über die Traumdeutung bei den Juden handeln Almoli, Amram, Lowinger," and in the bibliography of works before 1900 Freud listed "Almoli Salomo. Pitrôn Chalômôth. Solkiew, 1848." The only edition of Freud's German text available to me was the sixth edition, 1921, Leipzig und Wien. Strachey's English translation (New York: Avon, 1972) translates Freud's footnote; but in his translation of the bibliography mistakenly gives "Solomon" as Almoli's surname.

   Almoli entitled his work *Me'fasher Halmin*, but it has been usually published and referred to as *Pitron Halomot*. I have used the Warsaw edition of 1902 supplemented by the Cracow edition of 1580. The Warsaw 1902 text, except for an omission or two, to be noted, is the same as the Cracow 1580 edition. Unless otherwise designated all quotations are from the Warsaw 1902 edition. Grünbaum, op. cit., cites various editions and abridgements, e.g., Calcutta abridged edition of 1848.

2. Yalon in his "Chapters . . ." includes a photograph of page 24 of Almoli's proposal.

3. *Interpretation of Dreams*, p. 3

4. Ibid., p. 4.

5. Ibid., p. 5.

6. Grünbaum, op. cit., considers Isaac Abrabanel's (1437-1508) comments to Genesis 40–41, where he discusses Joseph's dream interpretations, "the

foundation" of Almoli's book. Grünbaum also refers to Almoli's use of the pseudo-Hai Gaon Dream Book and his use of the comments to Genesis 41, by the Gaon Samuel ben Hofni (d. 1013). In passing Grünbaum adds that both Abrabanel and the Gaon "drew on the works of the Greek philosophers." Almoli says that he read "gentile books." And, here and there, he makes specific references to non-Jewish authors. He refers to Aristotle's *On Sense and Sensible Objects* and *On the Soul*, to *The Lives of Eminent Philosophers* (presumably by Diogenes Laertius), and to the legends of the Greeks (it is unclear as to whether this is a title). Almoli mentions Averroes (1126–1198), the Muslim commentator to Aristotle, whom he read or heard about through the translations of Gersonides or other Jewish translators; he also mentions Al-Ghazali (1058–1111), Persian Muslim theologian translated into Hebrew by Abraham ibn Hasdai (early thirteenth century), and Avicenna (980–1037), the Muslim philosopher.

Of Jewish works, Bible and Talmud and their commentaries were of crucial importance for Almoli. Of medieval Jewish thinkers, Maimonides, *The Guide*, and Gersonides, *Wars of the Lord* were important. He refers to the *Zohar* quite frequently and on occasion to *Akedat Yitzhak* by Isaac Arama (c. 1420–1494), Spanish rabbi, thinker, preacher, first published in Salonika, 1522. He also quotes the following rabbinic authorities: Mordecai ben Hillel ha Kohen, "The Mordecai" (1240?–1298); Nissim ben Reuben Gerondi, "The Ran" (1310?–1375?), one of the most important Spanish talmudists; Solomon ben Abraham Adret, "The Rashba" (1235–1310); Yom Tov ben Abraham Ishbilli, "The Ritba" (1250–1330); Asher ben Jehiel, "The Rosh" (1250–1327); Moses Nahmanides (1194–1270), Spanish talmudist, kabbalist, commentator to the Pentateuch; Eleazar ben Judah of Worms, "The Rokeah" (1160–1238); Shem Tov ibn Shem Tov (c. 1380–1441), rabbi and kabbalist; Abraham ben Samuel ibn Hasdai; Moses ben Jacob ibn Ezra (1055–after 1135), Hebrew poet and philosopher; David Kimhi (1160–1235), grammarian and exegete; Abraham ibn Ezra (1092–1167), poet, grammarian, and exegete; and other medieval Jewish commentaries.

7. *Interpretation of Dreams*, p. 4. The verse is Isaiah 29:9–11.

8. Ibid., p. 6.

9. Ibid., p. 6. *Tikkunim* is a technical term, plural of *tikkun*, which can be translated as "restitution," "reintegration"; it can refer to "an order of service for certain occasions" (*Encyclopaedia Judaica*, Glossary).

10. Ibid., p. 44.

11. Ibid., p. 3.

12. Ibid., pp. 7–8. The sage's statement is in *Nedarim* 38a.

13. *Responsa from Heaven*, ed. Aaron Marcus (Tel Aviv, 1957). I. M. Ta-Shema's study of *Responsa from Heaven* in *Tarbiz* 57:1 (Oct.-Dec. 1987): 51–66 and Neil Danzig's study "Geonic Responsa, . . ." which also analyzes *Responsa from Heaven* in *Tarbiz* 58:1 (Oct.-Dec. 1988), discuss very important issues. But whatever the original composition of *Responsa from Heaven* and whatever the later additions may have been, a question of consequence, what we quote is relevant no matter who wrote what.

14. Cf. *Sefer Yetzirah*, with commentaries (Jerusalem: A. S. Monzon, 1962), chap. 4, pp. 100–101. Elijah ben Solomon Abraham ha-Cohen (d. 1729) of Smyrna in his *Midrash Talpiyyot* (New York, n.d., photo-reprint of 1860 Czernowitz edition), pp. 184a-b, transcribed a number of ways for eliciting dreams. Abraham Hamoy devoted an entire book, *Ledrosh Elohim* (Leghorn, 1879) to techniques for eliciting dreams.

15. *Interpretation of Dreams*, p. 8.

16. Ibid., pp. 12–13.

17. Ibid., p. 11.

18. Ibid., p. 19. *Berakhot* 57b is the source of the quote within the quotation.

19. Ibid., p. 20.

20. Ibid., p. 21.

21. The conventional translation of *hakham* is "wise person," i.e., "sage"; *navon*, "one who understands." According to tractate *Hagigah* 14a, "one who understands one thing from another" (Soncino translation to which there is an added footnote, one "who is able himself to draw conclusions on the basis of the knowledge imparted to him"). *Hakham* and *navon* occur in Genesis 41:33, 39, and are used by Joseph and Pharaoh.

22. Almoli attributed this view to Isaac Arundi (first half of the fourteenth century) and quoted from Arundi's commentary to Job, which survives only in manuscript. Cf. *Enc. Jud.*, vol. 3, col. 412.

23. *Interpretation of Dreams*, p. 22. The term *ba'al halom*, "Lord of the Dream," a supernatural dispenser of dreams, is used only twice by Almoli. Surprisingly, it is found only twice in the Babylonian Talmud (cf. *Ozar Leshon ha-Talmud*, vol. 8, Hebrew, by Ch. Kasowski [Jerusalem, 1959], p. 694). Almoli says nothing about *ba'al halom*.

24. *Interpretation of Dreams*, p. 25.

25. Ibid., p. 25.

26. Ibid., p. 36.

27. Ibid., pp. 37–38.
28. Ibid., p. 42.
29. Ibid., p. 44.
30. Almoli quotes Proverbs 1:6.
31. *Interpretation of Dreams*, p. 68.
32. These statements are from *Berakhot* 55b and 55a.
33. Cf. chapter 2, "Dreams in *Sefer Hasidim*."
34. *Interpretation of Dreams*, p. 21.
35. Ibid., pp. 47–48.
36. Ibid., p. 48.
37. Ibid., p. 44. The quote within this quotation is from 1 Samuel 3:1.
38. *Berakhot* 55b.
39. *Interpretation of Dreams*, p. 34.
40. Ibid., p. 35.
41. Ibid., p. 16. In *Berakhot* 55b, it is seven days.
42. *Berakhot* 55b.
43. *Interpretation of Dreams*, p. 27.
44. Ibid., p. 49. The rabbinic quotation is from *Berakhot* 55b.
45. Ibid., p. 31.
46. Ibid., p. 49.
47. Ibid., p. 51.
48. Ibid., p. 53.
49. Ibid., p. 76.
50. *Shabbat* 11a. Soncino's translation modified.
51. *Interpretation of Dreams*, p. 83.
52. Ibid., p. 86.
53. Ibid., p. 86.
54. Ibid., pp. 88–89.
55. Ibid., p. 92.
56. Cf. chapter 6, "Dream Therapy in Jewish Tradition" for this and the Priestly Benediction.
57. *Interpretation of Dreams*, p. 100.
58. *Nedarim* 8a–b.

59. *Interpretation of Dreams* (Cracow, 1580), p. 104.

60. Oppenheim, *The Interpretation of Dreams in the Ancient Near East*, p. 219.

61. Ibid.

62. *Interpretation of Dreams*, p. 6.

63. Oppenheim, *The Interpretation of Dreams in the Ancient Near East*, p. 219.

64. *Interpretation of Dreams*, p. 11.

65. *The Interpretation of Dreams in the Ancient Near East*, pp. 207, 209. The quotation within the quotation is from Numbers 12:8.

66. *Interpretation of Dreams*, p. 56.

67. Ibid., p. 92.

68. Cf. above, n. 6.

69. *International Encyclopedia of the Social Sciences*, vol. 14, "Dreams" (New York: Macmillan Company and The Free Press, 1968), p. 267.

70. *Interpretation of Dreams*, p. 4.

71. Complete: Warsaw, 1902; in part, by Meir Backal in his *Sefer Pitron Halomot ha-Shalem* (Jerusalem: n.p., 1965), which is not complete and lacks all scholarly apparatus.

CHAPTER 4

1. Only the second edition of *Minhat Yehudah* (Jerusalem: Safra, 1955–56) is available to me. This edition has under the title on the front cover the words, in Hebrew, The Spirits Tell. In his introduction, Ftayya noted that he had gathered his material by 1912 and implied that he had then begun working on his commentary to Hayim Vital's *Tree of Life*. But "only now in 1933 [that the commentary is finished]" is he working on *Minhat Yehudah*, which was first published in Baghdad in 1933. All translations are mine.

   I have used the Library of Congress transliteration of the author's surname, in Hebrew *PTYYA*, rather than Fetaya.

2. P. 2.

3. P. 31.

4. P. 34.

5. P. 35.

6. Pp. 32–33.

7. P. 33.

8. P. 34.

9. Ibid. The verse from which he quotes is Numbers 5:21 and concerns the suspected wife.

10. Ibid.

11. P. 35.

12. Ibid.

13. Ibid.

14. Ibid.

15. P. 61.

16. Pp. 36–37. Ftayya did not comment on the fact it took place before "the *three* days" of his interpretation.

17. P. 37. "Gehinnom is not only for punishment but also for purgatory." *Encyclopaedia Judaica*, vol. 13, col. 83.

18. P. 38. *Gematria* "consists of explaining a word or group of words according to the numerical value of the letters." *Enc. Jud.*, vol. 7, col. 369.

19. P. 38.

20. P. 39.

21. Ibid.

22. Ibid.

23. P. 61.

24. P. 116.

25. Ibid.

26. Pp. 71–73.

27. Pp. 121–122.

28. Pp. 125–126.

29. Pp. 75–76. Isaiah 30:33: "For a hearth is ordained of old; Yea for a king it is prepared, Deep and large; the pile thereof is fire and much wood." *Hemdat Yamim* is "a major 18th century work of homiletics and ethics . . . the author is unknown and the question of authorship remains one of the great mysteries of Jewish bibliography. One fact remains clear, though some scholars have questioned it in recent years, namely that the author is a Shabbatean." *Enc. Jud.*, vol. 8, cols. 320–321.

30. P. 76.

31. Pp. 76–78.

32. P. 78.

33. *Berakhot* 55b.

34. *Minhat Yehudah,* pp. 82, 85–96, 109–113.

35. *Jewry of Iraq: Dispersion and Liberation, In Remembrance of Rabbi Yeheskel El Wakil,* ed. Abraham Twena (Ramala: Geoula Synagogue Committee, 1968), p. 45.

36. Ibid.

37. David Solomon Sassoon, *A History of the Jews of Baghdad,* trans. and pub. by his son David S. Sassoon (Letchworth, 1949).

38. *Jewry of Iraq: Dispersion of Liberation* (Supplement to Book Seven, Addenda and Errata, Books 1–6), ed. A. H. Twena (Ramala: Geoula Synagogue Committee, 1973), p. 24.

39. *Jewry of Iraq: Dispersion and Liberation, In Remembrance of Rabbi Ezra Dangoor,* ed. A. Twena (Ramala: Geoula Synagogue Committee, 1973), p. 22.

40. *Jewry of Iraq: Dispersion and Liberation, In Remembrance of Rabbi Yeheskel El Wakil,* p. 59.

41. *Bet Lehem Yehudah,* vol. 1 (Jerusalem: Kozlovski, 1969), p. 1b.

CHAPTER 5

1. *Pitron Halomot oder Troym Buch* (New York: The Hebrew Publishing Company, 1907). All the quotations from this book are my translations from the Yiddish. I am grateful to Marshall Wolke of the Spertus College administrative staff for his helpful suggestions in translating some Yiddish terms.

2. A. B., despite my efforts, remains unknown. He did not simply translate Solomon Almoli's *Interpretation of Dreams.* He knew it; he borrowed from it. But he composed his own *Interpretation of Dreams.* I refer to him as A. B. throughout this book.

3. Ibid., p. 3. I have intentionally transliterated *dazein* because of the importance in our time of the concept *Dasein. A Dictionary of the Yiddish Language,* comp. Alexander Harkavy (New York: The Hebrew Publishing Company, 1898), gives two meanings for *Dazein* – Existence and Presence. The quotation "A portion of the divine from above" that A. B. uses to refer to the soul is from Job 31:2 where, of course, it does not refer to the soul. My friend Professor Raymond Weiss suggests that this may be a

neoplatonic concept. Could A. B. have encountered this in his readings, perhaps in some medieval Jewish text?

4. Ibid.

5. Ibid., p. 4.

6. A. B.'s notion of a king's dream derives from *Midrash Rabbah, Genesis,* chap. 89, ¶4, "a king's dream embraces the whole world." Cf. *Midrash Rabbah, Genesis,* vol. 2, trans. H. Freedman (London: Soncino Press, 1961), p. 822.

7. *Pitron,* p. 4.

8. Ibid.

9. Ibid., p. 5.

10. Ibid.

11. Ibid., pp. 5–6. The talmudic quotation is in *Berakhot* 55b. I have translated *his* Yiddish translated quotation from the Talmud. He has taken some liberty with the text.

12. Ibid., p. 6.

13. Ibid., p. 7. The quotations are from *Baba Batra* 12a and *Berakhot* 55b, respectively. Each Hebrew quotation is also parenthetically translated into Yiddish; the second quotation is also interpreted in Yiddish. I assume that A. B. knew the tractates and pages in which they occur.

14. Ibid.

15. Ibid. The quotation "Life and death is in the power of the tongue" is in Proverbs 18:21; but A. B. reversed the first two nouns and added the Hebrew prefix to *tongue.*

16. Almoli, op. cit., p. 58.

17. *Pitron,* p. 9.

18. Ibid.

19. Ibid., p. 10.

20. Ibid.

21. Ibid., p. 11.

22. Ibid., p. 12.

23. Ibid., p. 13.

24. Ibid., p. 15.

25. Ibid.

26. Almoli, op. cit., p. 65.

27. *Pitron*, p. 16.

28. Almoli, op. cit., p. 66.

29. *Pitron*, p. 16.

30. Ibid., p. 17.

31. Ibid.

32. Ibid., p. 19.

33. Ibid., p. 20.

34. Ibid.

35. Ibid.

36. Ibid., p. 21.

37. Ibid., p. 22.

38. Ibid., p. 23.

39. Ibid., p. 24.

40. Ibid., p. 25. The Talmud's interpretation is in *Berakhot* 57b.

41. *Pitron*, pp. 28–29. I have not been able to identify the source of this story or that oneirocritic.

42. Ibid., p. 29.

43. Ibid., pp. 29–30.

44. Ibid., p. 30.

45. Ibid., p. 31.

46. I have found no bibliographical references to this work. The traditional scholars I have consulted who would know of a book with so traditional a title had never heard of it. A. B. refers to the source of the story in a misleading manner. He writes, "The *Baal D'shaynim V'Raananim* tells the following story." This is a standard orthodox formulary for the author of a traditional book, which is used in place of the author's proper name. A. B.'s introduction to the story leads one to assume that the story is in that book; but A. B. has actually said only that the author of that book had told a story. S. Simonsohn's *History of the Jews of the Duchy of Mantua* (Jerusalem: Kiryat Sepher, 1977) has no reference to Esperero of Mantua.

47. *Pitron*, p. 32.

48. Ibid.

49. Ibid., p. 31.

50. Ibid., p. 4.

51. *History of Religions* 31:1 (August 1991): 39–59, at 39.

CHAPTER 6

1. The section on the Priestly Blessing in this chapter was published in a somewhat different version in the chapter "The Priestly Blessing: A Prayer Concerning Dreams" in my *Exodus and Exile: The Structure of the Jewish Holidays* (Minneapolis: Fortress Press, 1992), pp. 79–84. For the Priestly Blessing, see Numbers 6:24–27 (Jewish Publication Society Bible, Philadelphia, 1917).

2. The translation is that of *The Daily Prayerbook, Translated and Annotated with an Introduction by Philip Birnbaum* (New York: The Hebrew Publishing Company, 1949), pp. 628–632, modified by me. The primary source for this text is tractate *Berakhot*, p. 55b. There are minor differences between the talmudic text and the prayer book text. There are also liturgical additions in the prayer book.

3. Erwin Straus, *The Primary World of the Senses* (New York: Free Press of Glencoe, 1963), pp. 278, 288.

4. Oppenheim, *The Interpretation of Dreams in the Ancient Near East*, p. 226.

5. Straus, op. cit., p. 278.

6. Hans Jonas, *The Phenomenon of Life* (New York: Delta, 1966), p. 137.

7. Jacob ben Asher, *Tur Orah Hayyim*, vol. 1, part 1, "Laws of Raising the Hands" (Tel Aviv: Ester, 1964, photo offset), p. 113b; Joseph Caro, *Shulhan Aruch*, vol. 1, part 1, "Laws of Raising the Hands" (Tel Aviv: Ester, 1977, photo offset), p. 81b. Note also the commentaries on each page.

8. J. D. Frank, *Persuasion and Healing* (Baltimore and London: Johns Hopkins University Press, 1973, revised ed.), p. 165.

9. Jonas, op. cit., pp. 144, 154.

10. Cf. Zeligman Baer, *Seder Avodat Yisrael* (Berlin: Schocken, 1936, photo offset), pp. 578–579. Many current editions of the traditional prayer book do not include this text. The primary source of this text, without the medieval additions, is tractate *Berakhot*, p. 55b. *Amelioration of Dreams* is my translation for the Hebrew rubric *Hatavat Halom*.

11. Literally, "Who love him," *ohavim oto*.

12. *Encyclopaedia Judaica*, vol. 4, "Beth Din and Judges" (Jerusalem, 1973).

13. *Berakhot* 55b.

14. Menahem ben Solomon Meiri (1249–1316) in his gloss to *Berakhot* 55b, would have the dreamer tell his dream to the other three. Cf. *Bet Ha-behirah* to *Berakhot* (Jerusalem: Makhon Ha-Talmud, 1964), p. 205.

15. We quote, throughout, the Jewish Publication Society Bible translation (Philadelphia, 1917) with occasional modifications in order to make explicit the Talmud's observations.

16. See previous note.

17. The standard English translation is in somewhat different order from the Hebrew.

18. These are posttalmudic additions.

19. These are standard phrases, the first clause made famous by virtue of inclusion in the Day of Atonement liturgy. Cf. Baer, op. cit., p. 579, for bibliographical notes.

20. See n. 18.

21. Frank, op. cit., p. 165.

22. Cf. H. D. Halevi, "The Raising of the Hands," *Shevilin* 19 (1967): 123.

23. J. Pedersen, *Israel: Its Life and Culture*, vol. 1 (London: Oxford University Press, 1946), pp. 182, 198, 199.

24. Frank, op. cit., p. 20.

25. S. J. Korchin, *Modern Clinical Psychology* (New York: Basic Books, 1976), p. 129.

26. Quoted in Korchin, op. cit., p. 284. He did not give the source for this statement.

27. I base this on the Talmud's interpretation of the Name, *Berakhot* 9b, which is also quoted by Rashi on Exodus 3:14. The usual "I am," and its variations, is based on Maimonides' interpretation who was, obviously, fully aware of the Talmud's interpretation. The Jewish Publication Society edition of *The Torah*, 1962, transliterates the Name and has a footnote accounting for this. S. D. Goitein in his *Iyyunim B'Mikra* (Tel Aviv: Yavneh, 1957), chap. 5, offers another interpretation that also implies "personal involvement" in contrast to the medieval, now uncritically accepted, metaphysical interpretation of the Name.

28. Cf. Korchin, op. cit., p. 287.

29. Cf. Almoli, op. cit., p. 100; *Shulhan Arukh*, ¶130, p. 84b, the gloss and the

commentaries. Meir ben Simeon Ha-Me'ili (first half of the thirteenth century) had suggested this be done in the absence of the Priestly Blessing. Cf. *Sefer ha-Meorot*, ed. M. Blau (New York: n.p., 1964), p. 169.

CHAPTER 7

1. *Berakhot* 55b.

2. *Berakhot* 56a.

3. Ibid.

4. A. Steinsaltz is of the opinion that these dreams were told to Bar Hedya over a period of many years. Cf. his edition of tractate *Berakhot* (Jerusalem: Israel Institute for Talmudic Publications, 1967), p. 246.

5. *Berakhot* 56a, Soncino translation.

6. Ibid., Soncino translation.

7. *Sefer ha-Meorot*, ed. M. Y. Blau (Brooklyn, NY, 1964), p. 168, my translation.

8. *Sanhedrin* 30a.

9. *Horayot* 13b.

10. *Gittin* 52a. In each reference the Hebrew phrase is the same; but each translator of the respective Soncino volume gives a different connotative translation and in a footnote adds a denotative translation. For tractate *Sanhedrin*, Jacob Shachter's translation "Dreams have no importance for good or evil" is supplemented by "Neither raise nor lower." For tractate *Horayot*, I. W. Slotki's translation "Dreams are of no consequence" is supplemented by "Words of dreams neither bring up or down." For tractate *Gittin*, Maurice Simon's translation "Dreams are of no effect one way or another" is supplemented by "Words of dreams neither cause to ascend or descend." I prefer Slotki's translation.

11. A. Grünbaum, "Pitron Halomot, History and Sources," in *Areshet*, vol. 4, pp. 180–201, at p. 191. He notes, however, that there is a reference to the Amelioration of Dreams service in the *She'iltot* of Ahai, the section on Joseph's interpretation of Pharaoh's dreams.

12. Ibid.

13. *Beit ha-Behirah*, vol. 2, ed. S. Dickman (Jerusalem: Makhon ha-Talmud ha-Yisraeli ha-Shalem, 1964), pp. 205–206.

14. I. Epstein, *The Responsa of Rabbi Simon B. Zemah Duran* (London: Oxford University Press, 1930), Preface.

15. *Sefer ha-Tashbatz*, part 2 (Lemberg, 1891; Tel Aviv, photo offset, n.d.), Responsa no. 128 and no. 129.

16. Ibid., Responsum no. 159.

17. *Magen Avot* (ha-helek ha-shelishi, Livorno, 1785; Jerusalem 1969, photo offset).

18. Ibid., p. 71b.

19. *Encyclopaedia Judaica*, vol. 3, col. 958.

20. *Magen Avot*, p. 72b.

21. *Perush ha-Rashbatz al Berakhot*, ed. D. Z. Hillman (Bnai Brak: Makhon Aznaim la-Torah, Israel, 1971).

22. *Sefer ha-Hezyonot*, ed. A. Z. Aescoli (Jerusalem: Mosad Ha-Rav Kook, 1954).

23. This attempted justification in ¶52 was, according to Aescoli in his footnote on pp. 80–81, in ¶1 in earlier editions. Aescoli was to explain this in a promised study of Vital's book, which he was unable to produce before he died.

24. *Shevilin* 6: 18–19 (1967): 114–128.

25. I rely on Ch. J. Kasowski, *Otzar Leshon ha-Talmud*.

26. Cf. Eliezer ben Yehudah, *Milon ha-Lashon ha-Ivrit*, vol. 14 (Jerusalem: H. E. Benyehuda, 1951–52), p. 6871 and fn. 1.

27. *Encyclopedia Talmudit*, vol. 7, cols. 84–91. Authors of articles are not identified.

28. Cf. n. 10.

29. *Encyclopedia Talmudit*, vol. 7, col. 84, my translation.

30. Ibid., cols. 86–87.

31. In nn. 10, 34, 35, 46, 48, 55, 60, 61, 71.

32. *Encyclopedia Talmudit*, vol. 8, cols. 753–756.

CHAPTER 8

1. In *Sukkah* 43b; *Mo'ed Kattan* 18b; *Gittin* 5b twice; *Hullin* 106b; *Avodah Zarah* 30a.

2. Cf. H. Yalon, *Pirkei Lashon* (Jerusalem: Mosad Bialik, 1971), p. 222, n. 15.

3. *Minhat Yehudah* (Jerusalem, Safra, 1955), p. 126.

4. *Encyclopaedia Judaica*, vol. 2, col. 867.

5. Brooklyn, NY: Mesorah Publishers, 1987.

6. Ibid., p. 697.

7. Edited with translation by Rabbi Jules Harlow (New York: Rabbinical Assembly, 1985).

8. Ibid., pp. 472–474.

9. Chaim Stern, ed. (New York: Central Conference of American Rabbis, 1975).

REFERENCES

A. B. *Pitron Halomot oder Troym Buch.* New York: The Hebrew Publishing Company, 1907.

Abarbanel, Isaac ben Judah. *Perush Al ha-Torah.* Vol. 1. Jerusalem: Bnai Arbel, 1963.

Almoli, Solomon. *Helihot Sheva.* Ed. Henoch Yalon. Jerusalem: Mosad Ha-Rav Kook, 1944.

_____ . *Pitron Halomot.* Cracow: Jacob b. Naphtali of Lublin, 1580; Warsaw: Lewin-Epstein, 1902.

The ArtScroll Siddur. Trans. Nosson Scherman. Brooklyn, NY: Mesorah Publications, 1987.

Aubert, Vilhelm, and White, Harrison. "Sleep, A Sociological Interpretation." In *Sociology and Everyday Life,* ed. Marcello Truzzi, pp. 325–345. Englewood Cliffs, NJ: Prentice-Hall, 1968.

Avot de Rabbi Nathan. Ed. Solomon Schechter. New York and Philadelphia: Feldheim, 1967.

Backal, Meir. *Sefer Pitron Halomot ha-Shalem.* Jerusalem, 1965.

Baer, Seligman. *Seder Avodat Yisrael.* Berlin: Shocken, 1936 (photo offset).

Bar, Shaul. "Dreams in the Bible." Ph.D. diss., New York University, 1987.

Ben Asher, Jacob, *Tur Orah Hayyim*. Vol. 1, part 1. Tel Aviv: Ester, 1964 (photo offset).

Ben Jacob, Moses of Coucy. *Sefer Mitzvot Gadol*. Vol. 1. Jerusalem: S. Monzon, 1961. Reprint. Vol. 2. Munkacs: Kahn and Fried, 1905.

Ben Yehudah, Eliezer. *Milon ha-Lashon ha-Ivrit*. Jerusalem: H. E. Benyehudah, 1951–1952.

Bitel, Lisa M. *"In Visa Noctus*: Dreams in European Hagiographa and Histories, 450–900." *History of Religions* 31:1 (August 1991): 39–59.

Caro, Joseph. *Shulhan Aruch*. Vol. 1, part 1. Tel Aviv: Ester, 1965 (photo offset).

The Daily Prayerbook. Trans. Philip Birnbaum. New York: Hebrew Publishing Company, 1949.

Danzig, Neil. "Geonic Responsa *Sha'arei Teshuvah* and *Shelot U-Teshuvot min Ha-Shamayim*." *Tarbiz* 58:1 (October–December 1988): 21–48.

de Lorris, Guillaume, and de Meun, Jean. *The Romance of the Rose*. Ed. Charles D. Dunn and trans. Harry W. Ross. New York: E. P. Dutton, 1962.

Duran, Simon ben Zemach. *Magen Avot*. Part 3. Jerusalem: Mekor, 1969 (photo offset).

———. *Perush ha-Rashbatz al Berakhot*. Ed. D. Z. Hellman. Bnai Brak: Makhon Aznaim la-Torah, 1971.

———. *Sefer ha-Tashbatz*. Part 2. Tel Aviv: H. Gitler, n.d. (photo offset).

Encyclopaedia Judaica. Ed. Cecil Roth. Jerusalem: Keter, 1961.

Encyclopedia Talmudit. Ed. Solomon Zevin. Jerusalem: Mosad Ha-Rav Kook, 1959.

Epstein, Isadore. *The Responsa of Rabbi Simon B. Zemah Duran*. London: Oxford University Press, 1930.

Frank, Jerome D. *Persuasion and Healing*. Rev. ed. Baltimore and London: Johns Hopkins University Press, 1973.

Freud, Sigmund. *Die Traumdeutung*. Leipzig und Wien: Franz Deuticke, 1921.

———. *The Interpretation of Dreams*. Ed. and trans. James Strachey. New York: Avon, 1972.

Frieden, Ken. *Freud's Dream of Interpretation*. Albany, NY: State University of New York Press, 1990.

Ftayya, Judah. *Bet Lehem Yehudah*. Vol. 1. Jerusalem: Kozlowski, 1969.

———. *Minhat Yehudah*. Jerusalem: Safra, 1955–1956.

Gates of Prayer: The New Union Prayerbook. Ed. Chaim Stern. New York: Central Conference of American Rabbis, 1975.

Goitein, Shlomo D. *Iyyunim B'Mikra.* Tel Aviv: Yavneh, 1957.

Grünbaum, Aaron. *"Pitron Halomot:* History and Sources." *Areshet* 2 (1966): 180–201.

Ha-Kohen, Elijah. *Midrash Talpiyyot.* New York: L. Landau, n.d. (photo offset).

Ha-Me'ili, Meir ben Simon. *Sefer Ha-Meorot.* Ed. M. Blau. New York, 1964.

Halevi, Chaim D. "The Raising of the Hands." *Shevilin* 6:18–19 (1967): 114–128.

Hamoy, Abraham. *Ledrosh Elohim.* Leghorn: E. Benamozegh, 1879.

Harkavy, Alexander. *A Dictionary of the Yiddish Language.* New York: The Hebrew Publishing Company, 1898.

The Holy Scriptures. Philadelphia: Jewish Publication Society, 1917.

International Encyclopedia of the Social Sciences. Ed. David L. Sils. New York: Macmillan Company and The Free Press, 1968.

Jacob of Marvége. *Shailot uT'Shuvot min Ha-Shamayim.* Ed. Aaron Marcus. Tel Aviv: Hapoel Hamizrachi, 1957.

———. *Shailot uT'Shuvot min Ha-Shamayim.* Ed. Reuben Margulies. Jerusalem: Mosad Ha-Rav Kook, 1957.

Jewry of Iraq: Dispersion and Liberation. In Remembrance of Rabbi Ezra Dangoor. Ed. Abraham Twena. Ramala: Geoula Synagogue Committee, 1973.

Jewry of Iraq: Dispersion and Liberation. In Remembrance of Rabbi Yeheskel El Wakil. Ed. Abraham Twena. Ramala: Geoula Synagogue Committee, 1973.

Jewry of Iraq: Dispersion and Liberation. Supplement to Book Seven, Addenda and Errata, Books 1–6. Ed. Abraham Twena. Ramala: Geoula Synagogue Committee, 1973.

Jonas, Hans. *The Phenomenon of Life.* New York: Dell, 1966.

Kasowski, Chaim J. *Otzar Leshon ha-Talmud.* Jerusalem: Ministry of Education and Culture, Government of Israel and The Jewish Theological Seminary of America, 1954.

Korchin, Sheldon D. *Modern Clinical Psychology.* New York: Basic Books, 1976.

Kristianpoller, Alexander. "Traum und Traumdeutung." In *Monumenta Talmudica,* ed. Alexander Kristianpoller, pp. 1–67. Vienna: Harz, 1923.

Lieberman, Saul. *Hellenism in Jewish Palestine.* New York: The Jewish Theological Seminary, 1950.

Meiri, Menahem ben Solomon. *Bet Habehira to Tractate Berakhot.* Ed. Samuel Dickman. Jerusalem: Makhon Ha-Talmud Ha-Yisraeli Ha-Shalem, 1964.

Midrash Hagadol Bereshit. Ed. Mordecai Margulies. Jerusalem: Mosad Ha-Rav Kook, 1947.

Midrash Hagadol Shemot. Ed. Mordecai Margulies. Jerusalem: Mosad Ha-Rav Kook, 1956.

Midrash Rabbah Genesis. Trans. H. Freedman. Vol. 2. London: Soncino Press, 1961.

Midrash Rabbah Lamentations. Trans. A. Cohen. London: Soncino Press, 1961.

Midrash Shir Ha-Shirim. Ed. Joseph Chaim Wertheimer. Jerusalem: Ktav Yad Va-Sefer, 1971.

Midrash Tannaim al Sefer Devarim. Ed. Z. Hoffman. Berlin: Z. H. Itzkowski, 1908–1909.

The Mishna. Trans. Herbert Danby. Oxford: Oxford at the Clarendon Press, 1933.

Oppenheim, A. Leo. *The Interpretation of Dreams in the Ancient Near East.* Philadelphia: American Philosophical Society, 1956.

Pedersen, Johannes. *Israel: Its Life and Culture.* Vol. 1. London: Oxford University Press, 1946.

Price, Avraham. *Mishnat Avraham.* Toronto: G. Shepard, 1955.

Sassoon, David Solomon. *A History of the Jews of Baghdad.* Trans. David S. Sassoon. Letchworth: David S. Sassoon, 1949.

Scholem, Gershom. *Major Trends in Jewish Mysticism.* Jerusalem: Schocken, 1941.

Sefer Hasidim. Ed. Jehuda Wistenetzki and Jacob Freimann. Jerusalem: Wahrmann Books, 1969.

Sefer Hasidim. Ed. Reuben Margulies. Jerusalem: Mosad Ha-Rav Kook, 1957.

Sefer Yetzirah [with commentaries]. Jerusalem: S. Monzon, 1962 (photo offset).

Siddur Sim Shalom. Ed. Jules Harlow. New York: Rabbinical Assembly, 1985.

Simonsohn, Shlomo. *History of the Jews of the Duchy of Mantua.* Jerusalem: Kiryat Sepher, 1977.

Steinsaltz, Adin. *Talmud Bavli Berachot.* Jerusalem: Institute for Talmudic Publications, 1967.

Straus, Erwin. *The Primary World of the Senses.* New York: The Free Press of Glencoe, 1963.

Ta-Shema, Israel M. "Sheelot U-Teshuvot Min Ha-Shamayim." *Tarbiz* 57:1 (October–December 1987): 51–66.

Talmud [with commentaries]. Vilna: Romm, 1895.

The Tosefta. Ed. Saul Lieberman. Vol. 1. New York: The Jewish Theological Seminary of America, 1955.

Vital, Hayyim. *Sefer ha-Hezyonot.* Ed. A. Z. Ascoli. Jerusalem: Mosad Ha-Rav Kook, 1954.

Yalon, Henoch. "Chapters from R. Solomon Almoli's *Me'asseph le-Khol ha-Mahanoth.*" *Areshet* 2 (1960): 96–108.

_____. *Pirkei Lashon.* Jerusalem: Mosad Bialik, 1971.

INDEX

About the Author

Monford Harris, the author of *Exodus and Exile: The Structure of Jewish Holidays* (1992), has written numerous articles on dreams, various aspects of love and sexuality, and Jewish theology. Professor emeritus of Jewish thought at Spertus College in Chicago, Illinois, he holds a master's degree and a doctorate in Hebrew literature. He has also received rabbinic ordination. He and his wife, Rivkah, currently reside in Illinois. They have a son and a daughter.